T0078402

FROM GOD, EVERYTHING

REV. RICARDO MONTANO

WESTBOW
PRESS®
A DIVISION OF THOMAS NELSON
& ZONDERVAN

Copyright © 2022 Rev. Ricardo Montano.

All rights reserved. No part of this book may be used or reproduced by any means, graphic, electronic, or mechanical, including photocopying, recording, taping or by any information storage retrieval system without the written permission of the author except in the case of brief quotations embodied in critical articles and reviews.

This book is a work of non-fiction. Unless otherwise noted, the author and the publisher make no explicit guarantees as to the accuracy of the information contained in this book and in some cases, names of people and places have been altered to protect their privacy.

WestBow Press books may be ordered through booksellers or by contacting:

WestBow Press
A Division of Thomas Nelson & Zondervan
1663 Liberty Drive
Bloomington, IN 47403
www.westbowpress.com
844-714-3454

Because of the dynamic nature of the Internet, any web addresses or links contained in this book may have changed since publication and may no longer be valid. The views expressed in this work are solely those of the author and do not necessarily reflect the views of the publisher, and the publisher hereby disclaims any responsibility for them.

Any people depicted in stock imagery provided by Getty Images are models, and such images are being used for illustrative purposes only. Certain stock imagery © Getty Images.

Scripture taken from the King James Version of the Bible.

ISBN: 978-1-6642-7307-8 (sc)
ISBN: 978-1-6642-7308-5 (hc)
ISBN: 978-1-6642-7306-1 (e)

Library of Congress Control Number: 2022913087

Print information available on the last page.

WestBow Press rev. date: 07/19/2022

CONTENTS

PREFACE

In the final months of 2019, I coordinated with the pastor friend of mine, Bienvenida Fernández, who resides in Panama City, in Central America, to conduct a preaching campaign in her church in January 2020 and try to open a mission field in that area. We conducted the campaign between January 24 and January 26. The activity was a success, and the teaching reached the believers, so we decided that I would return in two or three months, as circumstances arose, to continue the work. But things went very badly as the Covid-19 pandemic began in March and all active projects had to be put on hold.

Amid that disconcerting situation, well into the year, without any possibility of ministerial development because of the order to close all public places, including the churches, I turned my face toward God and cried out, "What do I do now? How do I continue to serve you, Lord?" And I received from God, in my spiritual intuition, an inspiration that told me, *Write a book with the theological mindset that I have created in you.* From that moment on I took up the task of searching for, reviewing, and organizing the notes of the sermons, studies, and classes I had conducted during my ministry of preaching and teaching the Word of God.

The work of authoring the book began in December 2020, with all the difficulties, interruptions, changes, and revisions of the trade, and went until December 2021, when I finished the task entrusted to me by God.

The book *From God, Everything* does not intend to change the course of the history of Christian literature or to reveal theological secrets hidden until today. I only try to show a biblical theme, namely, holiness, and its development, from the ministerial point of view through which the Lord has guided me. It would be for me the greatest cause for rejoicing if in reading the pages of this book, the reader finds some teaching, wisdom, or joy that brings him or her closer to Jesus Christ, our Lord and Savior.

INTRODUCTION

Believing in God means much more than thinking that he exists. It also means turning him into a reason for being and into an experience of spiritual appreciation over all created things. God is essence and presence. The Bible explicitly states in many verses his actual existence, such as in, "Hear, O Israel: the Lord our God is one Lord" (Deuteronomy 6:4); "If my people, which are called by my name, shall humble themselves, and pray, and seek my face, and turn from their wicked ways; then will I hear from heaven, and will forgive their sins, and will heal their land" (2 Chronicles 7:14); and "For the invisible things of him from the creation of the world are clearly seen, being understood by the things that are made, even his eternal power and Godhead; so that they are without excuse" (Romans 1:20). But Genesis 1:1, which says, "In the beginning God created the heavens and the earth," is the principal among all because whoever is able to believe that God brought forth from nothing all that exists by the command of his voice is also able to believe everything else that the Bible says that God did, does, and will do.

To understand any story, it is necessary to know it from the beginning. The Bible is not exempt from this logical reasoning; therefore, we must comprehensively understand the events that occurred in the first three chapters of the Bible to correctly assimilate the rest of the history of the relationship between God and humankind.

The creation narrative contains subtleties that we must not

overlook, because they reveal knowledge about the way God works. A detailed reading of the first chapter brings to light two distinct facets of God's creative process: first, the impersonal creation, Genesis 1:3, 6, 9, 11, 14, 20, 24, where it is always shown that "God said," indicating that God commanded to do with the power of his Word, and second, the personal creation, Genesis 1:26, "And God said, Let us make man in our image, after our likeness," clearly showing that God personally participated in the formation of a man from the dust of the earth (Genesis 2:7). From this we understand that sometimes God commands things to happen by the power of his word, and at other times he acts directly to make things happen. We also see that God created all the natural elements out of nothing, but he created the man by "forming" him from the dust of the earth. That is, we are not creatures out of nothing, but we are creation formed from creation.

Now, Adam, the man formed directly by the hands of God, possessed and enjoyed holiness by way of creation, because everything that comes out of God's hands is holy. Eve, who was subsequently formed from Adam's rib, also enjoyed holiness by way of derivative creation. In this state of holiness—before disobedience—Adam and Eve knew only the good (Genesis 1:31). God endowed human beings with a brain of superior (rational) intelligence to communicate with him, and gave to them five natural senses, sight, hearing, smell, taste, and touch, to properly relate to the environment and subdue and maintain creation. Adam was the privileged being, the luckiest, because he had been instituted to rule creation. Everything was in his hands; he only had to obey God's instructions.

*

Scripture quotations are taken from the King James Version of the Bible.

CHAPTER 1

THE HUMAN DILEMMA BEGINS

It is important to pay special attention to the breath of life that God breathed into Adam's nostrils (Genesis 2:7) if we are to understand our existence and our likeness to God, and clearly discern the balance of the relationship between God and humankind according to the consequences of the events that were about to occur.

God possesses two types of attributes: the immanent, which consists of his omnipotence, omnipresence, and omniscience, and the relative or personal, which are intelligence, will, and feelings. After forming with his own hands from the dust of the earth Adam's human body, God bowed and breathed the breath (spirit) of life into him but in no way gave to him the divine spiritual essence that contains the immanent attributes of the Deity. God only gave him the energy of life with the relative or personal attributes of the Deity, with the purpose of establishing a close, communicative relationship with humankind, as happened in the garden of Eden while Adam and Eve remained in obedience. Our likeness to God is not divine but personal because we possess, by his grace and mercy, the same personal attributes of intelligence, will, and feelings. Because of this, we are the special creation of God.

Created with Purpose and Privilege

We were created out of love and with love, to love and be loved. The Bible declares that God is love, and the first condition is that love needs to be a blessing, which means it is to be given. A hidden love only causes suffering and frustration, but a shared love produces joy and satisfaction. This was God's purpose for creating humankind—to be the vessel of love, to receive and deliver this love, and to be a channel of extension of love, that intrinsic characteristic of the divine personality. We have the privilege of being God's chosen ones to continue the promulgation of his love for the world. God could have chosen eagles or lions to share his love, but he chose us. This is the first of God's choices for humankind. The whole of creation was designed with us in mind. We are the successful conclusion of God's work.

Up to One Day

An indeterminate amount of time after these marvelous events, Eve was walking in the garden, performing some of her daily tasks, and the serpent came to meet her. The Bible says that the serpent was cunning. To be cunning is to have the ability to use intelligence to profit from deception. And Satan is the father of lies (John 8:44). Obviously, since they lived in the harmonious creation that God had blessed, somehow Adam and Eve communicated with animals, though not with a formal language. That is the reason Eve did not run away when the serpent spoke to her. Let us be sure that this is the most fatal conversation that has ever taken place in the universe given its irremediable consequences.

Because of its importance, there are some aspects of the conversation and the environment in which it took place worth highlighting:

1. Eve knew the serpent. Temptation usually comes from something common or someone close (Genesis 3:1).

2. The essence of temptation is to question the truthfulness and authority of God's Word—in this case, "Thou shalt not die" (Genesis 3:4). This was a half-truth, which is the same as a total lie, because Adam and Eve died spiritually at that time, and physical death entered them and humanity.

3. Eve exchanged opinions with the serpent (Genesis 3:2–3). The only possible answer to temptation is a resounding no!

4. Eve tried to check Satan's insinuations and succumbed to them (Genesis 3:6). Sometimes it is better not to arrive in order to avoid going over; there are things that are better not to know.

5. Satan sent the serpent to speak to Eve because the one who had received directly from God the command not to eat of the fruit of the forbidden tree was Adam. Eve knew of the prohibition from the mouth of her husband; therefore, the serpent was much more likely to convince her.

The manifestation of the basic sinful cycle is relationship, doubt, temptation, and fall. Here we see it clearly: the serpent, who had a relationship with Eve, sowed doubt in the Word of God and presented her the temptation to make her eat of the forbidden fruit. Then Eve, who had a relationship with Adam, sowed in Adam doubt in the Word of God and presented to him the temptation by saying, "I ate and did not die, but now I know everything"—so Adam ate of the fruit of the forbidden tree. We must remain alert, because from our relationships will come doubt in the Word of God, presenting temptations with lies disguised as half-truths so that we fall into disobedience and sin.

This biblical passage is commonly used to claim the right to make our own decisions, with people stating that God has given us free will, but to do this is a mistake because free will does comes not from God but from Satan. God gave humans intelligence, will, and feelings to do good. The option of disobedience and conducting ourselves according to our own criteria comes from Satan, who, taking advantage of the relationship, sows doubt as a temptation to make us disobey. It was in Satan that the first known sin in the universe arose, when it was revealed against God, and it was he who introduced sin to humankind when he convinced Eve to disobey. She in turn dragged her husband into disobedience as well.

Sin is never an isolated event. The same pattern of relationship, doubt, temptation, and sin is always present, and the areas of temptation's influence are always the same:

1. The lust of the flesh ("For God doth know that in the day ye eat thereof" [Genesis 3:5a]).
2. The lust of the eyes ("Then your eyes shall be opened" [Genesis 3:5b]).
3. The pride of life ("And ye shall be as gods, knowing good and evil" [Genesis 3:5c]).

In 1 John 2:16, the apostle John said, "For all that is in the world, the lust of the flesh, the lust of the eyes, and the pride of life, is not of the Father, but is of the world."

This act of disobedience marked the end of humankind's perfect times and began the stage of debacle, separation, and death. God was pained in his holiness by the guilt of Adam and Eve, and he suffered, just as he suffers to this day for our sins.

Adam and Eve, made to reign, lost the holiness they possessed and became slaves to guilt and fear. The first change of attitude in them occurred. According to the Bible in Genesis 3:7, "And the eyes of them both were opened, and they knew that they were naked." The wrong thing here is not the opening of their eyes but their seeing of the undue. Here *naked* does not imply only lack of clothing; they had also lost rational innocence and spiritual holiness, diverting their attention from God to themselves and becoming aware of a new situation: *Oh, we are naked!* Really, they were unprotected because they had abandoned the assurance of holiness that comes from living within the divine will. Then, thinking for themselves while under the influence of the knowledge of evil, they tried to deceive God by using leaves to cover themselves, but this further manifested their fault because before, when they obeyed God, they had no need to cover themselves. Satan had promised them knowledge, but he really made them fools, because disobedience is always foolishness.

Ephesians 4:23 speaks of reversing this situation: "And be renewed in the spirit of your mind." Let us understand clearly what the Bible says. We must be renewed in the *spirit* of our minds, not in the *knowledge* of our minds. Adam and Eve, while they had in their minds the spirit of holiness, did not realize that they were naked, but after sinning it was the first thing they noticed because the spirit that governed their minds had changed. The attitude to temptation does not depend on knowledge but on the spirit that governs our minds, which is that which perceives and applies knowledge. Hence the need to renew "the spirit" of our minds, "by the washing of regeneration and renewing of the Holy Ghost" (Titus 3:5).

The first part of human history, which began in victory, ended tragically with the expulsion of the humans from the garden, destined to live on own their efforts and sacrifices and facing the consequences of their own actions. God offered everything to Adam and Eve, but they were not able to value it, so they lost the blessing they had enjoyed. This is a constant of the spiritual life: God offers everything to human beings, but we are unable to grasp the dimension and transcendence of divine things and do not give them the primordial place they deserve. We hear other voices that deprive us of the presence of the Holy Spirit. As a consequence, we must live by our own capacities, which are limited and do not provide the scope, security, and confidence that we could receive by remaining faithful to the Word of God.

The attitude of Adam and Eve was much more serious than disobeying; they also rejected God himself, telling him, "What we have is not enough. Your laws limit us. We want more, and we are going to take it, no matter what the consequences." God knew it, but he did not avoid it, because love is benign and suffers everything. Nothing hurts a father more than a child's disobedience and rejection, but there is also nothing more desired by a father than for his son to repent and return to him. That is God.

Pure and precious holiness, indispensable to maintaining a relationship with God and given with purpose and privilege to humankind on the day of their creation, had suffered the worst of fates. It was betrayed and abandoned to satisfy a curiosity that had already been announced as a tragedy: "But of the tree of the knowledge of good and evil, thou shalt not eat of it; for in the day that thou eatest thereof thou shalt surely die" (Genesis 2:17). The first known sin is pride, which arose in Satan and caused him to be rebel against God. It was also this same pride that Satan made enter Eve to lead her to disobey. That is why humility is so important in the character of the Christian: it inspires him or her to obey.

The holiness that satisfies and brings joy, and the love of God that made emotion and feelings accessible to the human soul, was outraged in the place where it was to prevail. The divine attributes were lost because of bad decisions. Nothing of God dwells in the wrong things. God is perfect, and only excellence pleases him.

Everything that comes from Satan provokes deception, guilt, accusation, and excuses. Adam excused his guilt by lying, accusing first Eve of offering the fruit and then God himself, because it was he who had given him the woman as a companion. Next, Eve lied, excused herself, and accused the serpent of seducing her to eat the forbidden fruit. But guilt and responsibility for sins committed is always personal. External influences, whatever they may be, by way of obedience to God's Word can be rejected and neutralized. Obedience is often breached because of a lack of control over impulses. Our emotions, when attacked, cause us to suffer a lack of foresight of the consequences. We are all exposed to temptation, but we are not bound to disobedience. Sin can be avoided, and God glorified.

To Be like Does Not Mean to Be Equal To

Genesis 3:22 says, "And the Lord God said, Behold, the man is become as one of us, to know good and evil." God knows evil but does not practice it; therefore, the knowledge of good in God is clean, not contaminated with evil. Humankind knows good, but we contaminate it with the evil we practice. That why God is holy and the human being is a depraved sinner.

Humankind is *like* God, because we know good and evil, but we have not been, nor are we, nor will we ever be *equal* to God, because we practice the evil that God rejects. Therefore, Adam and Eve had to leave the garden and enter an arid and inhospitable territory where our provisions had to be caught.

The consequences did not take long to manifest: suffering, loneliness, sadness—all the pains fell one by one on the earth, breaking the good and holy balance. The earth was filled with betrayal, death, and revenge. Humanity grew without God, increasing in violence, immorality, and savagery.

From then on, the history of the relationship between God and humankind can be summed up in the struggle between good and evil, light and darkness, God and Satan. Human existence lost God's joy and became marked by an effort to regain holiness to restore God's original purpose for humankind, to dwell in his presence forever. The human story of the recovery of eternal life is still being written, and we do not know how many more chapters remain to be told, but the truth is that one day the last chapter will be written by Jesus.

Humankind went against God in defiance of him and turned away from him, ignoring him, so that Jehovah decided not to contend with human beings anymore because their wickedness was great. He repented of having created them, and he set out to erase human beings from the face of the earth. "But Noah he found grace in the eyes of Lord" (Genesis 6:1–8).

Noah: Lucky Man or Chosen Man?

Human beings multiplied on earth because it was God's plan for humankind to "bear fruit and multiply; fill the earth, and subdue it" (Genesis 1:28), but they ignored the divine plan to establish a kingdom of peace and love on earth. Humankind without God lives governed by their animal nature, which limits the rational functioning of the brain in favor of responding only to the most primitive need of the human being: subsistence. In this way, men and women, abandoning the spiritual relationship with God, had degraded their lives to the exclusive satisfaction of fleshly desires. The situation they had reached was intolerable; a decision was imposed; and amid chaos and sordidness, God decided the most effective thing known to eradicate evil, that is, to uproot it. Genesis 6:6 says, implying with all intent and consequence, "And it repented the Lord that he had made man on the earth, and it grieve him to his heart." And Genesis 6:7 ends by saying, "For it repenteth me that I have made them."

Our modern word *repentance* comes from the Hebrew term *nachan*, which means "to relieve; to comfort," and from the Greek term *metanoia*, which means to change one's mind. When the Bible says that God "repented," it does not mean that he would annihilate humanity, but that he would alleviate the land of sin that oppressed humanity by using people with different ways of thinking and acting. God does not destroy his plans, his goals, or his revelations, but he is able to identify when the initial project has taken an incorrect path from which it is not possible to achieve the desired objectives and therefore must be renewed. For something to be revived, it first must be stripped of that which is old and useless. There was no hate in God's repentance, but love, because every intention to end evil to establish good is an act of goodness. Thus, repentance is manifested as undoing evil to establish goodness, comfort, and relief for those oppressed by sin by changing their way of thinking so that they can start a life with new hope. God did not repent of having made humankind, but of the evil that had developed in them. God did not intend to sweep humanity from the face of the earth, but to end the sin of humankind and to restore good using a new human generation. That is why we read in Genesis 6:8, "But Noah found grace in the eyes of the Lord."

The word in this verse that I want to highlight is *but* because this is a but of God, which is distinct from human buts. A human but functions as an excuse to shirk responsibility, which is why we often hear phrases like, "I understand your situation, but I can't do anything"; "I understand your pain, but it is not within my reach to solve it"; or "We have knowledge of what happened, but it is not within our radius of action to provide any relief." In conclusion, human buts are the predicate for excuses, in addition to being negative and insensitive, and are the cause of discouragement and frustration.

On the other hand, God's buts manifest themselves by providing all the resources of help and solution, pouring out God's goodness with his wonderful power over every obstacle that gets in the way of our spiritual life, regardless of our mistakes, faults, or responsibilities. God's but declares that, despite our sins, our faults, and our disobedience, he forgives us, restores us, adopts us, and makes us new creatures and will accompany us in all our struggles so that victory is on our side. The but of God is an attitude of comfort, relief, and blessing, saying, *Despite all that has happened, I am your forgiver, your protector and strength, and your Good Shepherd, and I will be will you until the end of days.* A but of God means that action, help, and fulfillment has come to manifest as a glorious blessing, because all good comes from God and the throne of grace. There is no shadow of evil in him.

The fact that Noah found grace in God's eyes is another sign that repentance in the foregoing verse refers only to humankind's wickedness and not to humankind itself. If such were not the case, then Noah and his family would have perished in the Flood as well. God fixes the defects; he does not destroy the cause. Where sin abounds, grace abounds (Romans 5:20).

Human beings descended from Adam abhorred God, but there was a person among them who attracted the attention of the Lord, not out of curiosity but out of attitude. Noah was the great-grandson of Enoch, the one who walked with God, grandson of Methuselah and son of Lamech, and had received from his ancestors the testimony of creation, the Fall, and the promises and deeds of God and kept them in his heart to obey them. Also he knew the prophecy given to his father Lamech, "This same shall comfort us concerning our work and toil of our hands, because of the ground which the Lord hath cursed" (Genesis 5:29), pronounced on him when he was born. It was not by chance that Noah was there; it was on purpose. In philosophy there is a concept known as causality, which states that chance or coincidence does not exist, but that every event has a previous cause that provokes it. Applying this concept to theology, we can say that nothing happens by chance or coincidence, but by "cause," namely, God's will and purpose. Our "causality" is God's plan established by his will. That place of perdition was the perfect setting for Noah's obedience to stand out. For light to shine, it needs a dark background.

God does not choose people for his work according to appearances, but according to potential qualities that only he can see. Noah found grace in Jehovah's eyes for his obedience, based on testimonies of God's deeds by his ancestors, manifesting the faith that was in him. This is the importance of testimonies: the one who listens to them, believes them, and obeys them is saved. Noah challenged those of his time to be faithful to God. He knew what God expected and was sure he would come. That is why God chose him to begin, from his offspring, another human generation that was faithful an obedient and separated from all evil.

By no means was Noah merely a lucky one. From birth he was a chosen one. God's elect have the privilege of finding grace in Jehovah's eyes by their obedience, their faithfulness, and a fear of God that have demonstrated in their behavior. If Noah had obeyed the voices of his ancestors, then how much more would he have obeyed the voice of God? This was an indispensable requirement that the person chosen to continue with God's plan must have, because the method that God would use was totally unknown to humankind and demanded a faith to obey without hesitation, because the people in Noah's day had no point of reference to judge from and had to trust that things would happen just as God had declared. In society we have a saying: "When in doubt, abstain." But in the life of faith, it must be said, "When in doubt, believe!"

The task entrusted to Noah was the greatest challenge theretofore known:

1. The never imagined, a flood.
2. The never seen, a great boat.
3. The never heard of, the end of sin.

We can imagine Noah asking God, "How I do it? Where do I start?" Then God revealed the answer to him: "Follow my instructions exactly." From there everything went according to plan under God's direction. The believer must build the ark of salvation for his or her own life by strictly following God's instructions. Let us ask God in prayer what we must do and that his will be revealed to us.

When the ark was finished, Noah entered with his wife, their children with their wives, and all the animals, "and the Lord shut him in" (Genesis 7:13–16). Let us try to imagine ourselves inside the ark when Jehovah shut the door. Then began the flood that lasted forty days, and then the waters remained one hundred fifty days on the earth, making a total of one hundred ninety days they had to wait until "the waters were dried up from off the earth" (Genesis 8:13). How did Noah and his family not go mad during that time locked in the ark, surrounded by all kinds of animals? Because that was where they were safe and secure. No matter how long or what we are surrounded by, if we are in God's safety and salvation, we will retain our personal and spiritual integrity.

The sinful generation given over to all kinds of aberrations had been eliminated, and thank God that the chosen man, his family, and animals of all species were again safe on earth, ready to begin the second generation of life pleasing to the Creator. Noah felt such immense joy at having been saved by God's grace that he immediately built an altar and offered sacrifices of pleasing aroma to Jehovah. Jehovah already knew Noah's obedience, but now he knew his thanksgiving and devotion, and that he had placed all his trust in him to rebuild creation and continue humanity.

The Bible says, "And the Lord said in his heart, I will not again curse the ground any more for man's sake; for the imagination of man's heart is evil from his youth; neither will I again smite any more everything living, as I have done. While the earth remaineth, seedtime and harvest, and cold and heat, and summer and winter, and day and night shall not cease" (Genesis 8:21–22). God was proclaiming his will for continuity for all created things despite his knowledge about the short- and long-term future, but everything was under his control. God would be compassionate toward humankind but not toward sin.

Noah and his sons were blessed, and they received the same mission that Adam was unable to fulfill: "Bear fruit and multiply, and fill the earth" (Genesis 9:1). A glimmer of hope shone on the divine horizon, considering the possibility that Noah might be able to achieve it. God was teaching the method of regaining holiness through obedience to his word. The holiness of creation that Adam and Eve possessed, but lost because of their disobedience, could be regained by the new generation descended from Noah through obedience. It was in human beings' hands to be reconciled to God by way of relationship. Obedience is relationship. Such a blessing seems incredible, but to the one who believes, anything is possible.

It is common to hear that God made a covenant with Noah, but it did not happen exactly like that. The Bible says: "And I, behold, I establish my covenant with you, and with your seed after you. ... And I will establish my covenant with you. And God said,

This is the token of the covenant which I make between me and you" (Genesis 9:9, 11–12). Jehovah never negotiated a covenant with Noah. God established, from his grace and mercy, an eternal covenant of forgiveness and salvation with humankind. God said: "The Lord is not slack concerning his promise, as some men count slackness; but is longsuffering to us-ward, not willing that any should perish, but that all should come to repentance" (2 Peter 3:9). God's eternal covenants are made according to his will because only he is eternal, and humankind enjoys him in the existential temporality of his life.

Determined and sure, Noah began to create a vineyard, which grew and fruited. And when the harvest came, the wine was made and everything was lost again. Noah got drunk and lay naked in the middle of his tent, and his son Ham came and discovered the nakedness of his father. New opportunities, the second beginnings we undertake with impetus, passion, and determination—but how long do they last? Often only a little time. From the right path we can emerge from difficulties or easy, as both consume our powers and our impulses in the same way, albeit in different fashions. Sometimes, the enjoyment of the result clouds our understanding and we make disastrous decisions. Other times, the effort we put forth and the sacrifices we make are so strong that we lose the original focus and obtain wrong results.

Sin is highly contagious. When we get close to it, it is quite easy to get infected. And it is never an isolated event, as we mentioned earlier. Here the same chain of events that unleashed the conflict in the garden of Eden was repeated: relationship (father, son), temptation (nakedness), and sin (Ham saw his father's nakedness). The man who had remained obedient to God in defiance of the lost society of his time, which earned him God's favor and trust, in reaping the first fruits of the blessing did not know how to turn them into thanksgiving as he did when he left the ark. The ark signifies salvation, the first fruits represents blessing, and worship would have ensured confirmation. But—and it is a human but, which is always used for purposes of excuse and abandonment—the continuation of humanity did not begin as it should have done. The sanctity that was to be regained was lost again. But—and here this is a but of God, which is always used for purposes of protection and hope—the die was already cast, and God was to continue his plan of forgiveness and salvation promised in the covenant that he had established with himself in relation to humanity. For the second time, humankind increased in number and spread throughout the land of defiance separated from God, living in according to their own criteria and convenience without caring about the divine will.

Human beings descended from the sons of Noah, who at that time spoke only one language, until they settled in the land of Shinar, forgot God, and began to build a city (according to their own laws) with a tower that would reach to heaven (their own God). They thought as God was in the blue sky they saw above them, they could get there to be on his same level, seeing what he saw and doing what he did.

The Tower of Babel represented humankind's rebellion, pride, and rejection of divine rules, even though those rules were what had saved them. There was no place in them for obedience and holiness. Only God in his infinite benevolence can endure such ingratitude. But sin is not an option on the salvation menu. Obedience is paramount in the relationship with God because it is intrinsically related to humility. The proud ones do not obey, only the humble do; and to establish God's plan of salvation on earth, humble men and women who obey the established rules are required. Those who are prideful and disobedient will never be members of the divine team.

Again, God mercifully intervened to save humanity from the deviations that separated them from the truth and confused their tongues by spreading them throughout the earth. The events related to the Tower of Babel cannot be taken lightly because they reveal an especially important spiritual principle in understanding the need for holiness and for rapprochement and reconciliation with God. This human group who had come to the valley of Shinar was the new generation that had no knowledge of sin because in the Flood, the sinful generation had disappeared. But even so, it arose from within themselves to do the opposite of the instructions they had received to fulfill God's statutes, which was given this time to Noah and his sons. What happened then? The answer can be found in Genesis 6:5 ("And God saw that the wickedness of men was great in the earth, and that every imagination of the thoughts of their hearts was only evil continually") and in Genesis 8:21 ("For the imagination of man's heart is evil from his youth"), and is confirmed by the apostle Paul in Romans 3:10: "As it is written, There is no righteous, no, not one." No matter where we come from or who we are, if we are human, we have inherited the sinful nature acquired by Adam and Eve, and that leads us unfailingly to be driven primarily to carnal and material impulses, discarding all spirituality or inclination toward God. This reality can be defined as follows: The human being does not become a sinner when he begins to commit sins, but even before he begins to commit sins, he is already a sinner by nature. A child, when it is born, without having yet even had a bad thought, is already a sinner because of the sinful inheritance that resides within it.

The apostle John categorizes this human defect in 1 John 1:10 in the following way: "If we say that we have not sinned, we make [God] a liar, and his Word is not in us." We should not try to circumvent our sinful nature, because it is simply impossible to do so; instead we must face it as an innate reality, one that we must submit to the obedience of the Holy Spirit. We are born evil, but God makes us good.

Humankind continued, incorrigible, but our tireless, immense, and powerful God, who gives to us with full hands, still had much to do and a long way to go. But what obstacle can stop God and his plans? What force can divert him if he is the energy and the power? He would go for more. More of the divine is not greater but better. Quality is more useful than quantity. A lot, if it is bad, does not work well; whereas good, if even only a little, fulfills God's plans. Many times, having more, we have less, and being less, we do more. The road was long, but it had to be traveled. Obedience and holiness had to be restored at all costs, for that is the divine method established for being in communion with God.

CHAPTER 2

ABRAM, THE MANIFESTATION AND CONSOLIDATION OF THE FAITH

Human beings are particularly good at growing and increasing but are unbelievably bad at faithfulness. Again, another group of human beings occupied the earth for its reins and with strife, focused on themselves. They believed that God's vast world belonged to them and that they could make fit their whims. Humankind persevered in sin, and God insisted on straightening their ways. Again Jehovah, of his grace and mercy, began the process of trying to regain the holiness lost in humankind. Noah's son Shem gave birth to Terah, and from Terah, Abram (Abraham) was born, and from the seed of Abram, God would create his chosen and beloved people.

Abram was born and lived in Ur of the Chaldeans, where he had married Sarai, who was barren. The Bible does not mention any exceptional quality in Abram that caught God's attention, as was the case with Noah, but God knew—and this is a but of God—what Abram was capable of. God does not seek ability, but availability, so he chose Abram.

Terah, whose name means delay, left the city of Ur of the Chaldeans carrying with him his son Abram with his wife Sarai, and grandson Lot, but they stopped in the city of Haran, which means barren, the last civilized city before entering the immense and dangerous Arabian Desert, where the land of Canaan was located. Because of his old age, Terah was in no position to undertake the hard journey, so they had to remain there until he died. God's work requires liberation from human limitations.

Everything related to Abram's life, mission, and ministry is extremely important because he is one of the most important people in the Bible. Abram was no better than his predecessors— he was full of fears and uncertainties—but God began to teach a new method of work to him, including follow-up, evaluation, and spiritual correction. Abram disobeyed, lied, and fled, but God did not abandon him, discard him, or punish him. Instead he instructed him and guided him in his ways again, making God's eternal purposes prevail over personal ones. God did not give Abram a mission as he did with Adam and Noah, "be fruitful, and multiply," but he promised him blessing ("And I will make of thee a great nation, and I will bless thee, and make thy name great; and thou shalt be a blessing" [Genesis 12:2]) and protection ("And I will bless them that bless thee, and curse him that curseth thee: and in thee shall all families of the earth be blessed" [Genesis 12:3]).

We too have promises of blessing in Christ Jesus, and we are sure they will be fulfilled at the right time according to God's plan. Abram's call was a process. He may have thought that Haran was the land God had promised him, but Jehovah appeared and reminded him that he had to continue to the land of Canaan. Nonetheless, Jehovah's mercy and goodness is greater than any human wrongdoing. Beyond all deviation, all mistakes, God's love never ceases to bring relief, comfort, and remedy for human setbacks inside and outside his work. From his essence flows to us the most beautiful source of forgiveness. God immerses us in his stream of living waters to quench our thirst and give us life in abundance. His forgiveness is what has brought us here.

Jehovah again entered the scene at the place of Shechem, where he appeared to Abram and gave him the right of ownership over the land of Canaan, and Abram built an altar to Jehovah there. Abram then continued to walk south, passing through Bethel, reaching the Negev. When a famine occurred in Canaan, he continued his journey to Egypt, far beyond the Promised Land—first, because he had not arrived (Haran), and now because it had been passed (Egypt). This is a quite common feature of human behavior: first, emotional gratitude for the euphoria brought about by forgiveness and salvation; then weakened conviction because of the wear and tear on one's energies from struggling with setbacks; and finally total abandonment, when the survival instinct surpasses the determination to please God. Whenever we go beyond the place, position, or situation that God has ordained for us, we enter the territory of defeat. Abandoning the area of promise weakens our spiritual integrity.

Adam was safe in the garden (his promised land) where God raised him, but after disobeying God, the first thing he felt was fear, which led him to lie. Noah was safe in the ark (his promised land), but when he emerged from it, he got drunk and provided the opportunity for the sin of his son Ham. Now Abram was leaving the Promised Land, and the first thing he experienced was fear for his life, for which he lied, saying Sarai was his sister, thereby putting Pharaoh at risk of committing adultery. This defines a pattern of spiritual behavior of abandonment:

1. leaving the blessing (the promised land),
2. feeling fear (because of a lack of security),
3. feeling the need to lie (because of lack of protection), and
4. creating a situation for sin (temptation).

The consequence of abandoning one's purpose is to be cast out. Although God had not made it public, he already had in his will the verse "For God hath not given us the spirit of fear, but of power, and of love, and of a sound mind" (2 Timothy 1:7). Abram did not know, but God did.

Transition

Each person has a measure of faith. The goal with that measure of faith is not to make it grow. In Luke 17:5–6, the apostles approached Jesus to ask him to increase their faith, and he did not answer them, "Receive a faith the size of the sun, the moon, or the earth," but instead he said, "If ye had faith as a grain of mustard seed—which is a tiny grain—ye might say unto this sycamine tree, Be thou plucked up by the root, and be thou planted in the sea; and it should obey you." Therefore, the main thing for faith is not its size but to exercise it with authority.

The first human beings who walked in the ways of God did so thanks to that measure of innate faith that is in all human beings, depositing within them the conviction that there is something beyond what we know. That intuitive faith placed them in the positions and situations desired by God, and although they were not perfect, they were sincere with themselves and with God. That elementary spiritual intuition was communicated to them as faith. But that is not enough. Faith cannot be limited to a spiritual intuition that shows us God's plans. It must be as defined in Hebrews 11:1: "Now faith is the substance of things hoped for, the evidence of things not seen," where there is no opportunity for doubt or for any possibility of error. This is only achieved with a profound transformation that embraces the entire existential essence of the human being.

This spiritual transition encompasses the three areas mentioned in John 16:8:

1. conviction of sin—recognition of behaviors contrary to God's will and plans;
2. conviction of judgment—internalization of the fact that God will judge all human beings;
3. conviction of justice—to know that the justice of God is manifested through the faith shown in obedience to God.

Abram had to be subjected to this process to regain lost holiness. The faith that is born within humankind is nourished by the carnal nature, and it is necessary to focus it on the spiritual dimension. The processes of spiritual change confront us with the harsh reality of the consequences of our actions. Abram would learn his lesson by going through strife and separation (Genesis 13), war (Genesis 14), reproach (Genesis 15), despair (Genesis 16), and renewal of the promise (Genesis 17).

Strife and Separation (Genesis 13)

According to God's instructions, Abram had to undertake his journey together with his wife, but in the first part of the journey he was also accompanied by his father, who stopped him in Haran, and his nephew Lot, who was now going to cause him setbacks and difficulties. More self-denial in favor of the purposes of God was necessary to achieve the required level of commitment, and to continue the process of salvation by way of obedience and sanctification proposed in God's will from the very moment of the Fall.

When Lot and Abram returned to the place where they never should have abandoned, the Promised Land, they found that there was not enough room for both to inhabit it together because they had many possessions. Abundance is not, as we believe, a blessing, it can also be the cause of strife and separation. It is fair to say that this situation was painful for Abram because only one thing had become clear: his love for Lot, whom he had always protected. Separations are painful and make an impact on the future. Split paths mean division for those who follow the wrong course, but for those who choose the right path, it means the beginning of new stages of growth. But this growth is not so easy to achieve, as it takes effort, tenacity, and dedication to consolidate the objectives.

Lot raised his eyes, which is a gesture of pride, and seeing the fertile plain of the Jordan, he failed to see the danger of perdition that lurked, namely, the end in Sodom and Gomorrah. For the second time Lot decided to leave Canaan. Abram remained in the Promised Land, a sign of his awareness of the importance of staying in the place where God had placed him, because that was where he would receive the blessing. We must understand that God has a plan that will materialize in the time according to his will.

Immediately after Lot left, Abram began to receive blessings. Jehovah said to him: "Lift up now thine eyes, and look from the place where thou are northward, and southward, and eastward, and westward, for all the land which thou seest, to thee will I give it, and to thy seed for ever" (Genesis 13:14–15). It is not the same to raise one's eyes interestedly to see what benefit, gain, or advantage one can obtain (as Lot did) as it is for God to make us look up so he may show us the blessing reserved for us (as happened with Abram).

War (Genesis 14)

But Abram and Lot's affairs would not end so simply. There were still things yet to happen. The kings of the earth threw themselves against Sodom and Gomorrah to attack those cities and plunder them, which they did. But by taking all the riches and provisions, they also took Lot and his goods. One of the survivors escaped and warned Abram of his nephew's fate, and Abram then enlisted his staff and went out to rescue Lot. This is how Abram, who was living in Canaan, the land that flows milk and honey, finally fulfilled in God and enjoying divine favor, became involved in a war that was not his, because of his nephew who had decided to expand his domain to Sodom and Gomorrah and had come to dwell within them, places of ignominy and immorality. Many of the wars before us are not our own; many of the battles we face we do not have to fight. These hostile situations are presented to us because of disobedience committed in the past. The importance of keeping our peace is to give God the opportunity to fight for us. Wars cause us to invest the resources we should be using in service to God in endeavors that cause pain and suffering. All our efforts should be focused on building for the kingdom and working out our spiritual salvation.

Reproach (Genesis 15)

Abram feared that the armies he had recently defeated would reorganize him and attack him to get revenge, but God told him: "Fear not, Abram: I am thy shield, and thy exceeding great reward" (Genesis 15:1). So all would be well. Human beings are very prone to living lives full of fear because of our limitations, but God tells us that the victory he will grant us is much greater than what we fear. "Fear not" is a very frequent affirmation in the Bible, speaking of God's protective relationship toward humankind in demanding situations and moments, because the Bible's purpose is to teach us that he is in control of everything and we can confidently rest in safety of his protection. Believers, when they convert to Christ, have defeated Satan's hosts of evil, and we know that Satan will tenaciously resist our conversion and try to attack us, but God repeatedly tells us not to be afraid.

Contrary to what we might expect, Abram reproached God: "What wilt thou give me, seeing I go childless, and the steward of my house is this Eliezer of Damascus?" (Genesis 15:2). How common are the reproaches when things do not go as we desire? Sometimes we disdain God for our not having received the things we think we deserve. But God does not intend to deny us anything, only to give it to us when it will be of blessing and profit. Abram was getting older and was not seeing the fulfillment of the promise. He was concerned about his family legacy, something particularly important in the biblical communities at the beginning of human history, and began to question the promise of God.

There are two types of doubt, one that rejects and one that wants. Abram's reproach did not indicate disdain for the promise. He required the promise because he desired it. He did not try to say, "Why don't you want to give me offspring? Okay, I do not care, I can live without any." Instead, his intention was a claim: "Why don't you give me offspring? I desire offspring; I need to have them to live." The consequences of the mistakes he had made in the past had caused him setbacks, but now he was beginning to move through a spiritual dimension of approaching the fulfillment of God's plans.

Memories should not torment us but should edify us with the teaching that comes through experience. To make a mistake is not to make a wrong decision that is unable to be rectified. We are never far from God, we only turn our backs on him, just turn around and stand in front of him.

Jehovah ended by saying that a son of Abram's would be his heir. He took him out outside and showed him the stars, and said, "This will be your offspring." And Abram believed the Lord and was made righteous. Our righteousness does not come about because of something we do but arises because of our belief in God.

Despair (Genesis 16)

Ten years had passed since Jehovah promised offspring to Abram and Sarai, and they were still childless, which discouraged them. They supplied the patience of faith with a longing of the flesh. To do this, they used a custom of their times, in which the servant sat on the legs of her mistress while the husband fertilized her. The son of the slave who was born from this union was considered as the son of the master. With this in mind, Sarai, who was barren, approached her husband and said: "I pray thee, go in unto my maid; it may be that I may obtain children by her" (Genesis 16:2). Abraham, interested and desperate to have offspring, thought that perhaps this was the method God was going to use to keep his word. By doing as his wife suggested, Abram had relations with Hagar, who conceived. But that was where the problems began.

Hagar felt more important than Sarai and despised her. What happened next? Sarai approached Abram and said: "My wrong be upon thee: I have given my maid into thy bosoms; and when she saw that she had conceived, I was despised in her eyes; the Lord judge between me and thee" (Genesis 16:5).

Disappointment and despair cloud our spiritual perception and makes us unable to recognize and identify God's plan to fulfill his purposes in our lives. Just because we have been waiting a long time for a response from God is no reason to follow counsel outside his Word. Above all things, the Word of God must always prevail.

Abram confused the method, and the consequences were not long in coming. He had a son, but from the impatience of the flesh—and all that is of the flesh causes problems and difficulties. His relations with Sarai were damaged. The family balance was broken, causing the rise of a nation that would subsequently cause great trouble for the people of Israel, and the birth of the son of promise was delayed. Whenever we try to advance God's plans using our own criteria, we will only succeed in delaying and complicating God's plan. Only patience brings fulfillment in God's perfect timing.

Renewal of the Promise (Genesis 17)

When one turns ninety, the expectation of the future does not go beyond the next day; therefore, no one has plans to be a father at that age. Only God, owner of time, life, and history, envisions the foundation of a people with purposes that are global and eternal in scope from a man of such advanced age.

The first verse of Genesis 17 reads, "And when Abram was ninety years old and nine, the Lord appeared to Abram, and said unto him, I am the almighty God; walk before me and be thou perfect" (Genesis 17:1). Epic in character, this verse contains a message and a demand:

1. The message is "I am the almighty God," making it clear that God had the ability, authority, and will to do as he wished, even against all logic, science, and nature, to fulfill his promises. The more improbable the fact, the greater the glory of God in the miracle.

2. The demand is "Walk before me and be thou perfect." Abram's process of spiritual growth was profoundly advanced, and God demanded to see the fruits of obedience and dedication, namely Abram's doing of God's will exclusively, because miracles occur and promises are fulfilled only by leading an impeccable life with a heart willing to sacrifice.

   "Walk before me" means "I will guide you," and "Be thou perfect" means "Obey completely."

Twenty-four years had passed since Jehovah made the original promise, and thirteen years had passed since the birth of Ishmael. Now Abram was ninety-nine years old. It is not possible to imagine a more suitable scenario for discouragement than this. But, and this is another *but* of God, when all seems to be lost, when there are no more opportunities, no more time, and no more strength, when everything humanly possible has been done and nothing has worked, when there is no more territory to advance, when all the doors have been closed by circumstances, and when we lie without hope, abandoned to whatever fate may come, God, the only one who assists without pretext the needy, the abandoned, and the desperate, appears with his light, his brightness, his radiance, his power, his strength, and his energy, radiating hope and joy, and filling souls with all satisfaction, which comes from the throne of grace. The God who resurrects the bones, causes the blind to see, causes the lame to walk, causes the deaf to hear, and causes the dumb to speak appears in all his glory and power to give, supply, and provide the long-awaited solution, the response, and the fulfillment of his promise.

"And I will make my covenant between me and thee, and will multiply exceedingly" (Genesis 17:2). This covenant has characteristics distinct from those of the eternal covenant after the Flood. At that time God established in himself, of his own will, a covenant of eternal durability with respect to land, humanity, animals, and all kinds of life. Now, God "put in," made a covenant with Abram aimed at covering the human temporality of Abram and his offspring. The covenant of Noah's time was universal and eternal, whereas now this covenant with Abram was limited to his offspring and the people who would be born from it. On many occasions when we refer to the Israelites, we say that they are God's chosen people, and this is true, but we might consider that there were multiple peoples in existence, one of whom were the Israelites, and God randomly chose them. But it is not so. The people of Israel did not exist. God made them arise, created them from the seed of Abram. The elect people of Israel means the people whom God made to be born for himself.

CHAPTER 3

THE FIRST PART OF THE PROMISE: THE SON

When "the time of life" was fulfilled, Jehovah visited Sarah (God had changed Sarai's name to Sarah), and Sarah bore Abraham (God had changed Abram's name to Abraham) a son. But during that "time of life," an event happened that deserves to be mentioned. One day when Abraham was sitting at the door of his tent near the holm oak of Mamre, the Lord appeared to him (Genesis 18:1). What happened next is one of the earliest biblical pieces of evidence of the divine Trinity.

In Genesis 1:26, the plurality of God is manifested by saying "Let us" make humankind in "our" image. It is clear with "let us" and "our" that in the act of humankind's creation, more than "one" intervened. But we do not know how many until we reach chapter 18, where in the first verse Jehovah appears to Abram; in the second verse, Abram raises his eyes and sees three men; and in the third verse, after prostrating himself before them, Abram says, "Lord." This pattern of exchange between one and three is a constant in this passage. In Genesis 1:26 we see the plurality of God, more than one, and here we see the quantity three. Then in the New Testament, the identity of each of them is revealed.

Another interesting consideration similar to what we read in

Genesis 18:3 is as follows: "And said, My Lord, if now I have found favor in thy sight, pass not away, I pray thee, from thy servant, this expression recalls But Noah found grace in the eyes of the Lord" (Genesis 6:8). And Noah, along with his family, was saved from perishing in the Flood. Here Abraham manifests the certainty (faith) that if he finds favor in God's eyes, God will not abandon him. This is an important characteristic of God's character: he will never leave behind, nor will he ignore, someone who finds favor in his eyes because of faithfulness, obedience, consecration, and surrender. Zacchaeus, wanting to see who Jesus was, climbed a tree to dodge the crowd, and Jesus first felt him, then saw him, and then, to save him, called him. God will never pass by when there is a needy person crying out, seeking his presence, relief, and comfort.

Sarah was already old when Jehovah made her conceive and have her own child. This promise was fulfilled because God is true to his word, not because Abraham and Sarah had properly obeyed. God always keeps his word because of his faithfulness, not our behavior. If it were because of our faithfulness, then God would be released from the commitment to honor his covenants and promises, because we always break the clauses set forth in the contract. The process of conversion that God began in Abram from Ur of the Chaldeans was reaching its fullness. No transformation of a disobedient person into a great man of faith takes but only a few days. The process of spiritual conversion requires time for spiritual work, years of trusting God in both trivial and transcendental moments to bring about change. Conversion is undergoing a challenge to establish the right.

But just as Abram had paid for the mistakes of the past regarding Lot, he now needed to pay for the mistakes of the past in relation to his son Ishmael, the son of human despair, born because Abram abided by social rules instead of waiting for God's perfect timing. Isaac was circumcised at eight days, as God had said, and was weaned at age three, as was customary, and then was celebrated in jubilation. But Sarah noticed that Ishmael was mocking her son Isaac and demanded that Abraham expel Hagar and Ishmael so that he would not inherit along with Isaac. The effects of the acts of the flesh endure and disturb the peace of the spirit.

Spiritual promises will never come true by following carnal methods or adopting carnal solutions. On the contrary, these will rob us of joy and communion, as well as hinder God's plans, creating strong feelings of contrariness and enmity. Customs do not change reality or maternal feelings. Given this situation, of course Hagar defended her son Ishmael and Sarah protected her son Isaac. Sarah was supposed to consider Ishmael her firstborn son and Isaac the younger brother, according to the hereditary order of that time, but this was not the case. When Isaac was born from her own womb as a fulfillment of God's promise, the configuration of the family changed. In no way would Sarah allow Ishmael to inherit the most and best of Abraham's estates now that she had had a legitimate son with him.

Abraham was sad because of the dilemma he faced. He had gone to Hagar because Sarah proposed the idea to him, not because it was his intention, just as Adam, without seeking it, ate of the forbidden fruit because Eve offered it to him. And both men spoiled the future. Adam spoiled the future of humanity in that his sin separated us from God, and Abraham, with his lust, helped create an enemy for the people of Israel, namely, the Ishmaelites. All offers that are not supported by the Bible must be rejected outright. Holiness demands zero opportunities for the enemy. Abraham loved Ishmael just as he loved Isaac, for they were both his sons, but Sarah rejected Ishmael because he was the son of Hagar the Egyptian servant. Instead, Sarah loved Isaac because he was her son, and she wanted the family goods to pass to him. But Abraham did not think of inheritance, but of love for his children and separation from the brethren, so he was disgusted and distressed by Sarah's request. What fault did Ishmael bear for the deeds of his parents? What was Hagar's fault in having been given to Abraham as a surrogate mother, she being a servant with no option to refuse? Obviously, none. The ones responsible for this cumbersome situation were Abraham and Sarah, and it was their job to correct the problem. Abraham wanted Ishmael to stay, and Sarah demanded that he leave. Divided opinions profoundly damage the conditions of development of the kingdom of God on earth. When opposing positions clash without seeking consensus, the tension created provokes harshness, resentment, and separation. These types of conflicts must be avoided at all costs, and for this to happen we must live in the will of God, who is the only one that provides fluidity, love, and unity. Abraham felt his Father's heart shatter.

We often fail to understand that God uses obstacles and trials to present opportunities and solutions. This characteristic of God is as real as it is frequently exercises. If, instead of pursuing dreams, we were to count the reality around us, we would discover that there is nothing more active in the world than the power and the will of God. Personally, when I remember the countless nonsensical and reckless acts I have committed, some of which accidentally put me in danger of dying, I realize that God's purpose for this day is what saved me.

A constant in God's attitude is his sensitivity to human suffering. He always arrives where a soul cries, a heart suffers, or a life hurts. And to this day he does the same. Here begins the final stretch, the supreme proof of Abraham's consecration as a friend of God and as the father of faith. Up to this point, the events in the history of the ministry of his growth in faith, obedience, and surrender had been related to his external environment, but now he would be hurt in the place where it would hurt him the deepest: his children, his blood, and his legacy. Abraham suffered, but God comforts, and his soft and precious word came to him with promises of care and prosperity, to provoke obedience, dispel fear, and facilitate the fulfillment of divine purposes. He already had had the experience of enduring consequences as a result of not following God's commands, and he knew that no matter how hard it seemed, what God arranged was always the best option.

The next day, Abraham prepared provisions for Ishmael and

Hagar, and with all the pain of his soul, but also with all the peace of God in his heart, he let them go. The man who in the past did not abandon his nephew, despite all the setbacks Lot had caused him and Jehovah's express command to leave his kin behind, had become an obedient servant through the spiritual process. And now we see him turn his son—closer and more beloved than a nephew—away, accepting God's will and his plan. Abraham's faith took the form of obedience and fulfillment.

The Supreme Proof (Genesis 22)

Abraham had separated from his first son, Ishmael, but he was certain that Ishmael would live because God had promised it, which comforted him. But the next test would be one of overcoming all possible human barriers, and if he were to surpass it, he would enter the pinnacle of faith and his name would be remembered forever and ever.

After many turbulent years, life passed peacefully for Abraham, and it seemed that at last all the vicissitudes were in the past. But the last step, to enter God's inner circle, was yet to be taken. Abraham was to go the extra mile of making a commitment to God and coming to understand that faith is above the prudence and caution recommended by the wisdom of experience. Our focus should not be on the promise but on the One who makes it. To pursue the promise as such is to walk by sight, but to focus on the One who makes the promise is to walk in faith. The human thought pattern dictates that in order to have more you must give less, but in spiritual reasoning the more you give, the more you receive.

God called Abraham: "And he said, take now thy son, thine only son Isaac, whom thou lovest, and get thee into the land of Moriah; and offer him there for a burn offering upon one of the mountains which I will tell thee of" (Genesis 22:2). Abraham's dismay must have been indescribable at this request. First, Jehovah said, "Take thy son Isaac." How was this possible when Abraham had another son, Ishmael? The explanation is simple: God had left Ishmael out of Abraham's offspring because he was the son of carnal despair and not the fruit of the patience of the spirit. Now the weight of the promise rested on Isaac, who had been conceived specifically to fulfill God's purpose.

So how does one make an offering in holocaust? There is a significant difference between sacrifice and holocaust as far as religious ritual is concerned. A sacrifice involves bringing a live animal to die on the altar, but with a holocaust, in addition to sacrificing the live animal, one must burn it completely before Jehovah. And to make things even more difficult for Abraham, the sacrifice of Isaac had to occur in a place that was a three days' walk away. All details were planned; God always has the future ready. The purpose of the three days was to give Abraham time to meditate on what was happening, where he was going, and what he was required to do, and then rationally decide whether God had the right to ask for the only child he had left.

Keep in mind that God could have commanded Isaac to be sacrificed where Abraham was, but sometimes the immediate orders give rise to a quick response that we later regret doing. A pastor recounted that he had conducted several evangelistic revival campaigns in his church and that the services of the campaign caused the church to be filled, with hundreds giving themselves to the Lord. But when the campaign ended, only two or three, and sometimes none, revisited the temple, because they had given themselves because of emotion, not because of conviction. In my younger years, every time I saw a Bruce Lee movie, when I left the cinema, I wanted to be a martial arts specialist, but the next day I forgot the matter. This sort of thing happens quite often. Under the emotional influence of the moment, we can commit acts that do not originate from a deep conviction. That is why God offered Abraham the opportunity to show the firm conviction of his faith, giving him time to pray, meditate, and decide.

The next day, Abraham set out to do God's will. Maturity is seen because it is shown. On the third day, Abraham lifted his eyes and saw the place from afar. These were three crucial days of solidification in the faith. Every day of the journey, waking up in the morning, walking throughout the day, and resting at night, Abraham was torn between returning (and keeping his son) and taking Isaac to the place of sacrifice and giving him to God, but he decided to continue to advance in obedience to Jehovah, understanding that God's will is the best that can happen. The expression "on the third day" is very noticeable because on the third day after his death, Jesus was resurrected, the eyes of the disciples were opened, and they perceived the reality of the kingdom of heaven. On the third day, the futile influence of emotion has disappeared and the conviction of what we must do becomes known. To the end, the faith prevails that convinces us of Jehovah's total right and authority over our human destinies.

It is no coincidence that in the land of Moriah there is also Golgotha, or Mount Calvary, where our Lord Jesus was sacrificed on the cross. It can be assumed that when Jehovah specified that Abraham to make the "burnt offering on one of the mountains that I will tell you," he led him to the very place of the crucifixion. Biblical history, which is the story of the relationship between God and humankind, abounds in allegories and symbolism of transcendental events that will (or would) happen later. Therefore, the events related to Isaac's sacrifice are the annunciation of what would happen to the Savior several centuries later. Before going to the appointed place, "Abraham said unto his young men, Abide ye here with the ass; and I and the lad will go yonder and worship, and come again to you" (Genesis 22:5). The phraseology in this verse is very eloquent: worship is a form of sacrifice; giving a child, presenting a son, and baptizing a son is a sacrifice of worship. Putting our destinies in God's hands, consecrating ourselves in body, soul, and spirit, and more than anything else following the teachings of Jesus in the gospels is a sacrifice of worship.

Abraham was to offer sacrificial worship in the form of obedience and total surrender, and finish saying, "And come again to you." Let us consider: Abraham did know that God would disallow Isaac's death. There is an antecedent in Genesis 18:17–18, where God revealed to Abraham that he would destroy Sodom and Gomorrah before doing so. Here the same thing could have happened, but then the sacrifice would not have made sense, because before doing the sacrifice he would have already known the result. Or, to consider another possibility, did Abraham have faith in Jehovah's mercy by recalling how he had saved Lot from the destruction of the two cities? Maybe. What we can be sure of is that after worshipping God in spirit and in truth, we will return safe from any sacrifice; Abraham had already learned this. God's plans are not fulfilled according to the circumstances that appear unexpectedly along the way but have been programmed into the design of the future since before the foundation of the world.

Having taken the wood of the sacrifice, Abraham had placed it on Isaac to be carried to the altar, just as Jesus carried the cross when he was to be sacrificed at Calvary in that same place. Abraham, who would serve as a priest, took the fire that purifies and the knife that executes. It was already decided: give to God that which belongs to God. "The Lord gave, and the Lord hath taken away; blessed be the name of the Lord" (Job 1:21).

"And they went both of them together" (Genesis 22:6). According to the geological data of the area where the Mount Moriah is located, the height is seven hundred forty-three meters, and although the Bible does not clearly state that they had ascended to the top, it is assumed that they must have climbed a considerable distance. Going together means much more than going side by side or in the same group; it means to be a compact and imbricated core advancing in the same direction and pursuing the same objectives. Abraham and Isaac were united in the same purpose of consummating one of the greatest acts of worship narrated in the Bible. There is little more beautiful than father and son voluntarily going to make a sacrifice out of obedience, one of them being the sacrifice and the other being the one to offer up his son. Likewise, Jesus suffered the cross to become obedient to the Father unto death—death on the cross (Philippians 2:8; Hebrews 12:2). Let us also go together in obedience to the Father until death, with the advantage being that we know the result.

"And Isaac spake unto Abraham his father, and said, My father: and he said, Here am I, my son. And he said, Behold the fire and the wood: but where is the lamb for a burnt offering?" A telling detail in this verse (Genesis 22:7) is the two ways in which the word *father* is used and differentiated. The first time is descriptive, narrating that Isaac spoke with Abraham, pointing to humanity, but the second time, the word *father* is perceived as supplicant and tender, denoting a reference to God. In his fears as a child, Isaac turned to his earthly father Abraham, but in the anguish of his spirit he cried out to the heavenly Father, Jehovah: "My Father." Jesus also, during the pain of his sacrifice, cried out to the Father, "My God, my God, why hast thou forsaken me?" (Matthew 27:46).

Abraham answered Isaac immediately: "Here I am, my son." The expression "Here I am" is found in at least seventeen passages of the Bible, and invariably, no matter what context it is in, it manifests an attitude of willingness to be obedient and to service in the manner of, *I am at your entire disposal for whatever needs to be done.* What wouldn't Abraham be willing to do for his son Isaac? Surely, he would want to offer himself as the victim of the holocaust in place of his son, but obedience implies following the instructions to the letter: *As God said, so it will be done.* Isaac was restless because he saw that there was fire and wood for the burnt offering but no lamb. He did not know it, but the lamb had been prepared in the bosom of the Father, waiting for his moment to be sacrificed for the salvation of humankind.

The next verse (Genesis 22:8) shows the other aspect of the father–son relationship: "And Abraham said, My son, God will provide himself a lamb for a burnt offering: so they went both of them together." Here the order of the two words in the expression "my son" is inverse to the previous verse, because it now accentuates the paternal protective aspect, assuring that God, the true Father, will provide him with the lamb, replacing insecurity with hope. We must know that when God provides for himself, he is also providing for us.

Arriving at the appointed place, Abraham built an altar, prepared the firewood, and placed Isaac on top, ready to make the sacrifice. How must have Isaac felt in such a helpless and desolate situation? How must have Abraham felt debating amid such a heartbreaking inner conflict? When so many feelings of sadness and pain are crowded at the same time and before a single fact and we are unable to find the explanation, solution, or way out, only from heaven can the provision come. Then the angel of Jehovah appeared, who was the same Spirit of Jesus before his incarnation in the womb of Mary. In theology these interventions or apparitions are known as theophanies or Christophanies. These miraculous ministries of Jehovah bring forgiveness, mercy, help, comfort, and salvation. He had previously appeared to Hagar twice, first to comfort her regarding Sarah and then to save Ishmael, and now he had come to deliver Isaac. Let us pray that the angel of Jehovah, incarnate in our Lord and Savior Jesus Christ, will appear in our lives to work miracles of forgiveness and salvation.

Then the angel of Jehovah sent voices from heaven to Abraham ordering him not to harm Isaac, because he had already proven that he feared God by not hesitating to give his only son as a sacrifice of burnt offering. The wording of this verse leaves no doubt that the angel of Jehovah and God are the same person when he says: "Lay not thine hand upon the lad, neither do thou any thing unto him: for now I know that thou fearest God, seeing thou hast not withheld thy son, thine only son from me. And Abraham lifted up his eyes, and looked, and behold, behind him a ram caught in a thicket by its horns: and Abraham went and took the ram, and offered him up for a burnt offering in the stead of his son" (Genesis 22:12–13).

The Bible teaches that everything points upward. The powerful voice of Jehovah's angel who brought mercy and forgiveness upon Isaac came "from heaven." Abraham raised his eyes, looked, and found a lamb locked in a bush by the horns, but was it possible that he raised his eyes and saw something that was on the ground? It was God who showed it to him, because all provision comes from on high, from the throne of grace, where Jesus is seated at the right hand of the Father. The reality is that the lamb was there from before they had come to the place to offer the sacrifice, but only after Abraham had demonstrated his willingness to give in sacrifice the most beloved and precious thing in his life, his son Isaac, was he shown the divine provision. Only when we sacrifice to God the most loved and precious areas of our lives will we see God's provision. He does not want to take anything away from us, just to know that we are willing to give it to him to obey his word and do his will.

"And Abraham called the name of that place, Jehovah Jireh: as it is said to this day, In the mount of the Lord it shall be seen" (Genesis 22:14). This is a statement of deep confidence that everything necessary will be supplied by God for his children. In our lives, the place where God will supply us is wherever "that ye present your bodies a living sacrifice, holy, acceptable unto God, which is your reasonable service" (Romans 12:1). Let us just trust him and hope in him.

Abraham had, at last, attained the state of holiness by obedience by following his faith. From this moment began the period of the practical realization of the fulfillment of the promise. God's work advances on grounds of spiritual holiness when one is in personal obedience. Also, now the faith took an empirical turn, based on evidence, on facts, and not only on spiritual intuition. Abraham is considered the Father of the Faith because he was the first to plant the facts that serve as the foundation for all subsequent acts of faith. In other words, Abraham's example is the basis of faith.

Faith in God is not fanaticism. Our faith is real because we do not believe in fairy tales or fables with morals, but in true historical facts. We have faith that Jesus will return for his church because he already came once to establish it, and if he came once, what could stop him from returning? Obedience to God should not be considered a nuisance, an obstacle, or a setback, but the only means of attaining holiness, which is the highest rung on the ladder to heaven and which means assurance of salvation and eternal life. Holiness is the harmonious integration of the gift of power of the Spirit, the gift of service, and the gift of the fruit of the Spirit into the life of the believer, placing him or her in unity with God, an anointed and victorious spiritual position, where God is glorified. In God's Spirit of revelation, the apostle Paul presented this attitude of faith: "I can do all things through Christ which strengtheneth me" (Philippians 4:13). This Pauline description speaks more of faith than of power, as is commonly believed, because faith in Christ is what makes everything possible. Spiritually, power is not our ability to do something, but the reality that is fulfilled in God's will.

A review of the life of Abraham takes us through the journey of a man who, dwelling in a place of pagan worship, began his ministry by spiritual revelation and who overcame countless inconveniences directed by God, who never let go of Abraham's hand. In this process of spiritual growth, Abraham went from misunderstanding to conviction and total submission. Abraham is an example of God's establishing the official method of regaining holiness by surrender and obedience to his will.

Isaac, the Facilitator of the Promise

The promise Jehovah had made to Abraham included a land (Genesis 12:1), a nation (Genesis 12:2; 13:14–16), and a son (Genesis 15:4; 18:10). During his life, Abraham dwelt in the Promised Land, Canaan, but did not possess it. Nor did he come to form a nation. He only saw the promise of the son fulfilled. So, shall we say that Jehovah failed to keep the promises he had made to Abraham?

Absolutely not. In every way God fulfill each of his promises, as he has always done, still does, and will continue doing. The reality is that the promises made by God to fulfill his plans and purposes are set forth in his vision of eternal time, with the plan possibly taking several human generations to materialize. Abraham received the son, and the son extended the promise to Abraham's grandson Jacob, from whom the nation of Israel was formed, who were the ones who conquered the Promised Land. In this way, Jehovah fulfilled his promises, but not all of them in Abraham's lifetime.

After the momentous events on Mount Moriah, Abraham returned with Isaac to his regular life in Beersheba. During this time, Abraham received news of the offspring of his brother Nahor. His wife Sarah died, and he married Keturah, who bore him six children, but all the inheritance belonged to Isaac, for he was the rightful son of the promise born of Sarah, Abraham's wife recognized by Jehovah as such. Isaac was not an active element in the continuity of the promise; he functioned as a facilitator of the stage whereon other actors would play the leading roles of the story. We are not all called to be "superheroes"; many will only be "heroes."

Isaac, like his father, and despite knowing his responsibility before God, left the Promised Land, which was his position in God's plan, and when difficulties arose, he lied to save himself (spiritual insecurity) when he felt he might be in danger because of the beauty of his wife Rebekah. But he was a faithful husband. In fact, he was the only patriarch who had a wife. He was also a man of prayer, who implored God to give him children, because like his mother, Sarah, Rebekah, his wife, was barren. God granted him his wish with twin sons, Esau and Jacob, which means a double blessing. It is important to highlight the biblical recurrence of barren women who prayed to God for children and, thanks to divine intervention, were granted children who fulfilled special parts of God's plan. These children, according to our understanding of the peoples in biblical times, were not considered "normal" but were marked with the favor of God. This is not to say that God, to enforce his divine plan, needs special people, but that he uses people willing to serve. Every believer has his or her position and mission in God's plan.

The birth of Esau and Jacob has a notorious particularity about it making it different and special. In a normal birth of twins, the two children are born with a certain time difference between them because there is a preparation period that lasts several minutes for the second child to settle and be placed in such a way to exit the vagina. But the Bible describes that Esau and Jacob were born at the same time since Jacob had his hand locked on his brother's foot. So they were not born separately, but united, one after the other, like a chain of two links. It is not the same behind as after. Seen in this way, it can be said that either of the two could have the right of primogeniture, but Esau was awarded first place in the order of childbirth, but not because there was a definite time gap between them to determine who was first and who second.

As adults, Esau became a hunter, and most of his time was spent hunting (materialism), whereas Jacob was more drawn to collective matters (spirituality). It happened that one day Jacob cooked a stew, and Esau returned from the field tired and hungry, asking his brother for something to eat, who proposed that he sell him the birthright in exchange for dinner. Forgetting the human inheritance and all spiritual responsibility, Esau sold his birthright for a plate of food, saying, "Behold, I am going to die; What, then, will the birthright serve me?" A common view of life among carnal people is that there is no other life after death; therefore they do not make any sacrifices thinking of the eternal life that God promises to those who give their lives to Jesus as Lord and Savior, with faith in the eternal and sufficient sacrifice that he made on the cross for the forgiveness of our sins, but they disdain salvation as something unreal. The Christian believer must have spiritual conviction of the kingdom of heaven and understand that only through Christ do we acquire our birthright, by being born of water and the Spirit, and being made new creatures and confirmed with adoption as children of God together with Christ. We must not despise our birthright, because it is the hereditary right to salvation together with Christ, the only begotten Son.

From this moment on the spiritual order changed in the continuation of God's promise, and Esau's place was now occupied by Jacob, who became the depository of the spiritual inheritance. As Isaac grew old, Jacob, in complicity with his mother, Rebecca, to avoid established social customs, used deception by wearing the clothes of his brother, Esau, to obtain the paternal blessing of the birthright, since he really the rights of the firstborn belonged to him because Esau had sold them to him. Jacob only maneuvered intelligently to be blessed with the right he had already bought.

In Abraham we see that Ishmael, the first son, was cast away because he was the son of the flesh, and the second son, Isaac, the son of promise, was the one who received the blessing of being responsible for continuing God's plan for his people. In Isaac we see how Esau, the firstborn, because he was born first, did not receive confirmation of his rights because he had sold them to his brother, Jacob, who was born behind him. What matters is not the natural position that touches us in life, but our willingness to assume the spiritual responsibility that God assigns to us. Regarding God's approval, being the first does not mean being the one, or being the one does not mean being the first, because it does not depend on numbers or position, but on consecration, faith, and obedience to God's will and submission to his plan. To be the one and the first, we cannot despise or sell our spiritual right as children of God acquired in the new birth in the spirit as children adopted by God. Therefore, we can only be one and first in Jesus, who is the only begotten Son of God, who is without number or position but is eternal, omnipotent, omniscient, and omnipresent, who never gave in and never sold or lost those rights. Only in Jesus can we claim our hereditary rights as firstborn sons based on the sacrifice of salvation he made on the cross to reconcile us to the Father through his blood.

Jacob, the Propitiator of the Promise (Genesis 28:3–4)

Abraham, after Sarah's death, took Keturah as his wife, with whom he had six children, but he made sure that all his personal property was received by Isaac. But in the spiritual sense we see that before his death, Abraham performed no action or ceremony dedicated to transferring or ceding the promise to Isaac. It happened as something natural, and in this continuity of the promise, Isaac performed no relevant act. He was a family man who only facilitated the next protagonists of the story, Esau, and Jacob.

It did not happen in the same way with Jacob. Legally, the rights of the promise did not belong to him, but he desired to realize them, and therefore he managed to acquire them. Isaac, his father, when he felt old and about to die, blessed Jacob by asking Jehovah: "And God almighty bless thee, and make thee fruitful, and multiply thee, that thou mayest be a multitude of people; and give thee the blessing of Abraham, to thee, and to thy seed with thee; that you mayest inherit the land wherein thou art a stranger, which God gave to Abraham" (Genesis 28:3–4). This gave him the blessing of the birthright, which represented acquiring not only the material goods of the family but also the responsibility of continuing the paternal legacy. Specifically, Jacob received the same promises that Abraham had received from Jehovah, a land, a nation, and a blessing. These promises were not a gift, but a task to fulfill the next step in the plan to establish God's holiness through the new nation that would arise by divine will. We might reproach Jacob's method of obtaining Isaac's blessing, but in this case a maxim is fulfilled that says the end justifies the means. Esau did not value spiritual ministry, but Jacob desired it so much that he did his best to attain it.

Confirmation of the Promise (Genesis 28:11–15)

Jacob's emotional state was unenviable: he had used his father, his brother wanted to kill him, and he was alone in the middle of the desert heading to his uncle's house to marry one of his cousins. Remember that Abraham sent his trusted servant to find a wife for Isaac, but now it was Jacob who must find his wife. It is known that when human paths end, the solution comes out of the sky. Jacob may have believed that his position was dubious because of the way he had obtained the birthright. He thought that God disapproved of what he had done, and he was consumed by insecurity. That is why he needed divine confirmation for himself and for others. How, without a divine revelation, could he be sure that what he was doing was God's will, and how could his offspring trust him as heir to the promise if God did not confirm him?

During one of the nights of the journey, Jacob went to sleep and received a dream of the greatest heavenly truth seen by a human being up to that time, a ladder that reached from earth to heaven. Previously, humankind had tried to reach heaven by building the Tower of Babel, but God interrupted the project because heaven is not reached by one's own will, but by divine permission. Jacob's ladder was a revelation that the earth is connected to heaven, from where Jehovah sends messengers to show his presence, intervene, and express his intention to engage in earthly human affairs, to enforce his sovereign and holy will among humankind. Confirmation manifested itself not because of Jacob's merits nor because of his ability to obtain the privileges of the birthright; it was thanks to the eternal love of God, committed to the restoration of holiness in humankind, to restore the lost communion.

As a result of this personal encounter with God, a new Jacob was born, totally committed to the fulfillment of the covenant. He said in his promises to God:

1. Jehovah will be my God (personal worship).
2. This place will be God's house (universal worship).
3. I will set aside tithing for you (thanksgiving).

Whenever we have an encounter with God, from that moment on everything will have a different meaning and significance. The world will become a whole new place after the new perspective is gained in that wonderful spiritual experience. God performs the miracle of disconnecting the visual nerve from our brain and connecting it to the Holy Spirit, to allow us to grasp the spiritual forces at work behind human actions. This is the true spiritual vision of the believer, to possess the gift of discernment of spirits (1 Corinthians 12:10).

CHAPTER 4

THE SECOND PART 2 THE PROMISE: THE NATION

Jacob continued on his journey and came to Haran, where his uncle Laban lived, to marry one of his daughters. But not everything went as desired, because God's plan was often interfered with by human decisions guided by material interests that created circumstantial conflicts and hindered the flow of spiritual purposes. Never by acting in the flesh will we obtain spiritual results. The only way the flesh and the Spirit can be united is for the flesh to be subdued to the Spirit. It is impossible to be 50 percent spiritual and 50 percent carnal, or to be 70 percent in the Spirit and 30 percent in the flesh. The only proportional possibility between the Spirit and the flesh in the believer is 0 percent carnal and 100 percent spiritual. Flesh and Spirit are incompatible. Let us abandon the flesh, which is separation and death, and live in the Spirit, who is communion and life with God.

After the required introductions, the necessary explanations, and the established affective relationships, Jacob fell in love with Rachel, Laban's youngest daughter, and dissolved her in marriage. But since he had no dowry to give, he offered Laban that he would work seven years for Rachel. After this time, on the wedding night, Jacob was deceived, and instead of his beloved Rachel, Leah, Laban's eldest daughter, was given to him, to fulfill the tradition of maintaining order from highest to lowest in the marriage of sons and daughters. However, after fulfilling his week of conjugal duties (honeymoon) with Leah, Jacob was also given Rachel, as was allowed by the customs of that time. But he had to work another seven years for Rachel. Jacob was confronted with the reality of life, working to obtain what he sought, trusting only to receive disappointments, and loving only to suffer. The happiness of the paternal home was left behind, and the task of building his own family, destined to become the people of God, began. In this new stage, Jacob began to have children, but his offspring were born amid rivalry, sterility, competition, and conflict.

Leah, the imposed wife, bore the first four sons to Jacob, Reuben, Simeon, Levi, and Judah. On the other hand, Rachel, the beloved wife, had no children because she was barren, and she was envious of her sister. So, making use of the custom of those times, she gave her slave Bilhah to Jacob to have relations with her, who gave her two sons, Dan and Naphtali. Seeing this, Leah gave her slave Zilpha to Jacob to have more children, and had two, Gad and Asher. In addition, Leah conceived two other boys, Issachar and Zebulun, and a girl, Dina, giving Jacob a total of eight sons and one daughter. In the end, Jehovah listened to Rachel's pleas and granted her two sons, Joseph and Benjamin. These are, in total, the twelve sons of Jacob, from whom the twelve tribes of the people of Israel were formed. If to this promiscuous and disorderly conduct that took place in Jacob's offspring we were to apply the pattern of divine discernment shown in Abraham's offspring with Sarah and Hagar, then we would see that the only children worthy of continuing in the formation of God's chosen people according to the promise would be Joseph and Benjamin, who were the only fruit of the relationship between the beloved wife Rachel, whom God pointed out, and Jacob, the depositary of the promise. But God does not change his goals; instead he adjusts the methods to achieve them. God's insistence on reinserting holiness in human beings is not a whim, it is an important requirement for the reestablishment of spiritual communion and personal relationship with him, because purity is the core of the whole function. Divine holiness emanates from the intrinsic pure, immaculate nature of the Deity, and nothing that is unholy is tolerable in his presence.

Jacob's sons had been born and raised in Haran. Now the new challenge to continue fulfilling the promise was to return to Canaan, the Promised Land, where Isaac his father dwelt, and settle there. But nothing pleasant to God was happening because, despite God's activities and presence in the lives of Jacob and Rachel, evil habits persisted. Relations between Jacob and Laban were extremely difficult, and the inconvenience caused movement. So, Jacob spoke to his wives Leah and Rachel and persuaded them to go out to Canaan, and then he received God's command: "And the Lord said unto Jacob, Return unto the land of thy fathers, and to thy kindred; and I will be with thee" (Genesis 31:3). But, and there is always a but, the procedure during the return was not the most appropriate. First, Jacob left the camp without warning Laban; the Bible says, "he fled," which was considered a hoax. Second, Rachel stole her father's idols, which is theft and idolatry. Third, as if Jacob and Rachel hadn't already done enough, their sons deceived and murdered all the men of the city of Shechem to avenge the dishonor Shechem, the son of Hamor, had committed against Dina their sister.

All the men God had used to try to restore holiness had failed. The biblical story of the people of Israel, their bad beginning, and their bad trajectory, just as God dealt with them to provide salvation on the cross of Calvary, is the same story as ours that, starting from the bad beginning and bad trajectory before we met Jesus, God gave us. It deals in such a way that it leads us to the cross of Calvary to receive the forgiveness of sins and to attain salvation and eternal life. Only God conceives of such plans.

Jehovah was immensely merciful to Jacob, and despite Jacob's lousy personal attitude, God sent him to Bethel to protect him from persecution and revenge from neighboring peoples. We may think based on the blessings we receive that God is pleased with us, but it really is God's mercy covering our faults and divine grace that we do not deserve being bestowed upon us. Jacob recognized how much benevolence and forgiveness had been bestowed upon him and demanded that his family and all those who had come with him remove the strange gods from among them, cleanse themselves, and change their garments to be able to offer a sacrifice to God (Genesis 35:3). These three actions make up the cycle of regeneration so that every believer is ready to offer himself or herself as "a living sacrifice, holy, acceptable unto God, which is your reasonable service" (Romans 12:1).

The process is as follows:

1. Remove the gods of others from among you.
   Eliminate idolatry. Idolatry is not just having representative images of other gods and worshipping them, but pursuing anything that captures your mind's attention and that causes you to dedicate yourself to it with more intensity than you dedicate yourself to God's presence. For example, your favorite artist, your favorite movie, your favorite car, the love you desire, or the happiness you seek, to name a few. Material things become idols when they go from being a mere belonging to being a preference. The believer must, before all things, love God, love whom God loves, love his or her neighbor, love the family of the faith, and finally love his or her enemies.

2. Cleanse yourselves.
   Although in the context of this biblical passage, the phrase "And cleanse yourselves" refers to the external cleansing of the body, what you really must do is not get dirty, so as not to have to cleanse yourself, the interior of your body, where the Holy Spirit dwells, so as not to grieve him. Spiritual cleansing is an internal process with an external projection. You cleanse what is given inside of you so that it is reflected

outside toward others. Daily bathing is hygiene, whereas inner cleanliness is holiness. That is what Jehovah demands of his people.

3. Change your dress.

The way you dress is a representation of your personality and character. The garments you wore before you met Christ respond to a nonspiritual ethic and aesthetic and belong to a time that should never have been, and you must eliminate all traces of that past. Your social appearance is the reflection of your inner spiritual life. A heart full of God, regenerated by divine wisdom and longing for the heavenly habitation, changes its personal appearance to please the Lord. If no change is observed, then no transformation has occurred. If you continue the same, Jesus has not entered your life.

Anyone would think that at last the seed of promise would take the path of holiness as the foundation for the formation of God's desired and chosen people, but this is only a hope. Jacob's married life was not holy, but promiscuous, provoking rivalry between his two wives, Leah and Rachel, and his two concubines, Zilpha and Bilhah, and between the twelve sons and the daughter he had with them. God in his infinite patience had a lot of work to do. Our failure is not about lack of knowledge; it is the result of our not trying enough. We know what the Spirit demands, but we still commit sins.

Finally, settled in Canaan, after reconciling with his brother, Esau, and having had his last son, Benjamin, to whom giving birth his wife Rachel had died, Jacob manifested a great preference for his son Joseph, creating a situation of jealousy with the other brothers, who sold Joseph to merchants who took him to Egypt. Although at this time no one could suppose Joshua was part of God's provisional plan for his people in the eternal vision of the saving promise for humanity.

Joseph's dreams teach something interesting; they show him

above his brothers, receiving the final concept of the plan, but not what would happen on the way to achieving it. The dream did not reveal that he would be a slave, that he would be falsely accused of attempted rape, that he would be imprisoned with no hope of freedom, that he would become the second most important person in Pharaoh's court, or that a famine would come and he would rise as the savior of the world of that time. The real revelation was that God would be with him. During the space of time we occupy in the universal physical dimension, we belong to God. Every second we live is by way of God's permission in the divine trajectory, for a specific task, as part of the strategy to facilitate the final goal. We all integrate into the plan where the facts of his will are accomplished.

In the approximately twenty years after Joseph was sold by his brothers and taken to Egypt, his life was a journey from the lowest to the highest, passing in between and through all the possible vicissitudes of a life of those who are called by God to commendable purposes. At this time, Joseph enjoyed authority and power, but God's blessing rested upon his life. Therein lay the secret. Then a famine ensued throughout the land, including the land of Canaan, and only in Egypt was there bread, as Joseph had foreseen thanks to divine revelation.

Moreover, during this time, because of Jacob's mourning for the loss of Joseph, his borrowed son, and the hidden guilt of his children, the unity of the patriarchal family had broken down, and the spiritual vocation for the fulfillment of the promise remained stagnant. In addition, they faced the danger of perishing by starvation, placing Abraham's seed at risk of disappearing. But Jacob possessed a fighting character forged in work to survive during the twenty years that he inhabited Haran the lands of Laban, his uncle and father-in-law, and when he heard that in Egypt there was food, he sent his children to go and buy food to survive. That is how God does things: no matter how far we go, we will always face the guilt of our evil deeds. Now the ten sons of Abraham would have to bow to Joseph. As much as they tried to change God's plan, everything was fulfilled to the letter.

Joseph couldn't be blamed if he had punished his brothers out of vengeance, but he chose not to. He did not occupy a prominent position for personal merit, but for God's specific purposes of salvation and for continuity at this stage of the promise. God's love prevails over all human feelings when it comes to his work, and the punishment of past evil deeds was not going to stop his promise. It was not time to settle accounts, but to open doors.

To fulfill spiritual goals, we must refrain from our personal passions, because the only way to love is to forgive. Joseph suffered, but the satisfaction of fulfilling a divine plan more than relieves all the pain suffered. Thus, Joseph's family, the seed of God's people, were received, served, and cared for in Egypt, where, moreover, Pharaoh allowed them to settle in the land of Goshen, and there they grew and prospered to become a great nation, coming to represent a danger—social, political, and economic—for the Egyptian empire. God had shown all these events in a dream to Abram (Genesis 15:12–16), and God does not lie.

CHAPTER 5

THE THIRD PART OF THE PROMISE: CANAAN

How is it possible that the one true God, the most powerful one, owner and Lord of all that exists, because he created it, allows the people he chose for himself to emerge in a foreign country and end up being slaves there? The answer is simple: because of their disobedience. God created human beings for the deliberate purpose of establishing and maintaining a personal and direct relationship with them based on terms of free will by obedience, but humans repeatedly broke the clauses of the established dealings, and that is what led them to slavery. Subsequently, they were separated from the divine blessing, and although God never changes the goal of his plan, he does change the methods and people chosen to achieve it. God fulfills his goals by teaching and guiding, making the justified and positive understood above the wrong and deviant. We must build, not destroy.

God's relationship with humankind through the ages has been a painful one. All kinds of grievances have occurred. Adam and Eve disobeyed out of vanity; Cain committed fratricide out of envy; Noah became intoxicated; and idolatry occurred at the Tower of Babel. Abram (Genesis 12:10–20), Isaac (Genesis 26:7), and Jacob (Genesis 27:6–29) used deceptive schemes to gain benefits for themselves. We could make an endless list of the mistakes of all human beings who have ever existed. That is why the Bible can be defined as the troubleshooting manual for the human race. Usually, a piece of equipment or an instrument will come with an instruction manual explaining how to make it work properly as designed. But the human being is a defective individual who does not function according to his or her original design. Therefore, God wrote a manual, not of operation, but of repair, where he points out human defects and teaches the divine solution to fix them, namely, obedience. The only way for good human functioning is through holiness, because in this way we were created and were designed to enjoy it. Outside of holiness everything is pain, anguish, and hopelessness, and a fierce darkness envelops us when we abandon it. Living in holiness is the most effective way to be happy and the only conceivable way to be saved.

The next man God used to continue his plan to recover the lost holiness was Moses. During turbulent times, when male children born to Hebrew women had been condemned to die at birth, God worked in such a way through Moses's mother and aunt that he could survive and grow up in Pharaoh's court. Why didn't God direct this mother to flee to a place outside Egyptian control, so that her son would be born free, and then use him to free the Israelites? Because in this way Moses would have grown free but ignorant, and ignorance is not helpful in God's work. That is why God organized things so that Moses could grow up in Pharaoh's court and learn the art of war and gain the knowledge necessary to lead, organize, liberate, and lead the Hebrew people on a pilgrimage through the wilderness. Training is particularly important because God cannot give us a task for which we have no prior knowledge to perform. We cannot receive a biblical message if we do not know the Bible. A sign of this in the New Testament is the apostle Paul. Why did Jesus not use any of the apostles who had been with him during his earthly ministry to theoretically ground the doctrine of the gospel? Because none was an expert in the law. God took Saul of Tarsus from the deepest and most ingrained sect of Judaism and made him Paul to place him at the top of grace because he possessed the knowledge necessary to conceptualize the transformation that is to happen in humankind to attain salvation. The first step in this process was an encounter with Jesus. Without knowing Jesus, it is impossible to understand the gospel.

Moses was raised in Pharaoh's court by his Hebrew mother, indicating that he knew both cultures, Hebrew and Egyptian, and knew of his family's Hebrew origin. Becoming a young man, he knew that one day he would walk among "his brothers" the Hebrews—which speaks of ethnic and cultural identification and inclination, because he might prefer the Egyptians and consider them his brothers, for having grown up within that culture. He saw an Egyptian beating one of the Hebrews, and then Moses killed the Egyptian and hid his body in the sand. Suddenly, the person God had in mind to bring his people out of slavery had become a murderer.

The next day, two Hebrews were squabbling with each other, and Moses said to the one who mistreated the other, "Why are you beating your neighbor?" The immediate answer was "Who has put you as a prince and judge over us? Do you want to kill me like you killed the Egyptian?" Moses loved his people, but they did not love him. Not all love is well reciprocated, no matter how good the intentions. It was time to get to safety, so Moses went to the land of Midian. Being far away geographically does not mean being far away spiritually. Although he turned away from Egypt, he did not abandon the feelings for the Hebrew people in his heart, and God took that into account. It is important to believe that traveling unknown paths is an experience that makes us depend on and seek the presence of God, who does not hide from those who need and seek him. This was the exact point at which the life of Moses was located: rejected by his ethnic people and persecuted by his adoptive people. When you feel that you have nowhere to go, look up. From there, an answer will always come.

Moses disappointed Jehovah, but Jehovah never disappoints himself because of the mistakes of the human beings he trusts. Anyway, it was not the first time this had happened, nor would it be the last. The divine choice is always to accomplish God's goals, realize his plans, and fulfill his purposes. With the passage of time, God's plans do not decay, they are consolidated and strengthened to be enacted at the right time. Meanwhile, Moses settled and prospered in Midian. The Israelites suffered in Egypt and cried out to God, who remembered his covenant with Abraham, Isaac, and Jacob. As he looked to them, he recognized them as the children of Israel, the beloved people of the promise.

Despite everything, Moses was destined to fulfill three great divine entrustments: first, to record the events that occurred from creation to the arrival of the Israelites at the entrance of the Promised Land; second, to deliver the people from slavery in Egypt; and third, to receive God's law at Mount Sinai and lead the Israelites through the wilderness to Canaan.

Spiritual location is critical to receiving divine vision in relation to the purposes of our lives. The Bible says that Moses carried a sheep through the wilderness and reached Horeb, God's mount. What better place to be than God's mount? It was so important that it was there Moses received the two main revelations of God, (1) the vision of the burning bush for the mission of his life (2) and the law for the subsistence as a nation of the people of Israel. Mount Horeb signifies divine revelation and guidance. Now, a bush appeared before Moses burning in fire. It caught his attention because it was not consumed. As he approached, the angel of Jehovah from a flame of fire said to him: "Do not approach; remove your footwear from your feet, because the place where you are is holy land." The image of this passage is precious. God's fire burns, but it does not consume; it heats, but it does not burn; and the radiance of God's flame sanctifies the place where we are located. The fire of God purifies the soul. Look for your burning bush so that God may manifest himself with the precise revelation that will lead you to a personal encounter with him, because that is what it is all about, meeting you again.

To be born free and to fall into slavery teaches you to value freedom, but when you are born a slave, you get used to slavery. That happened to the people of Israel. Even though they were in the majority, they accepted the Egyptian yoke. God had to come to save them because he is the only one capable of removing his children from the place where they are enslaved. Moses had an encounter with God, and it changed his life completely. The calm and happy future of a family life that he thought he awaited him became an existence dedicated to fulfilling God's plan. From that moment on he understood his mission as a chosen one, and although he considered himself humanly incapable, God showed him that things are possible not because of our abilities, but because of his power. From being a fugitive, Moses was turned into a liberator.

Moses submitted to God's will, obeyed all his commands, and freed the Israelites from Egyptian oppression, leading them for forty years through the wilderness until they reached Mount Nebo, in the fields of Moab, where he died, right near Jericho.

But during the journey, he disobeyed Jehovah's exact instructions in the wilderness at Zin, in the village of Kadesh, during a time of water shortage. Despite that, thanks to God's mercy, for one man's disobedience, the blessing of many was not lost. This is the same principle of salvation that Jehovah applied in the ministry of Jesus, which without regard for Adam's disobedience, by which humanity lost its holiness, he provided us, in Christ's perfect obedience, with the method for regaining it.

Moses's grievance was one of word and deed. Jehovah had told him to gather the congregation and, in front of them, to speak to the rock—then water would spout out to give the people and their beasts to drink. Moses obeyed, but not exactly as he had been instructed. He did as God said, gathering the people before the rock, then said, "Are we to make you draw water from this mountain?," arrogating glory to himself, not to God. Then, knowing that he had to speak to a girl, he hit her twice, doing it in his own way. Moses obeyed half-heartedly, whereas God demands total obedience. Moses did not lose salvation, but he lacked holiness, so that invalidated him to complete the mission of entering the Promised Land together with the people of Israel. Justice, obedience, and holiness are connected to each other. The Word is justice; obeying it is holiness; and holiness is the guarantee of completion of God's plans. Despite his eagerness, Moses failed God.

The journey of the Israelites for forty years through the wilderness, from Egypt to the land of Canaan, is a vivid illustration of the path to holiness. During that time, Jehovah purified the nation of Israel of their murmuring, idolatry, and rebellion. It was a long, hard, and sad process, but a necessary one. God had brought the people of Israel out of oppression, but they still showed reminiscences of slavery, which hindered their enjoyment of freedom, and when they faced some inconvenience, they wished to return to Egypt, instead of trusting in God and the promises he offered them. They were more concerned with the satisfaction of the flesh than with spiritual freedom. Although they had come out of slavery, they still missed it, which is a way of remaining a slave. We are not sanctified only by no longer sinning; it is necessary that we not desire to sin and that we reject it because it displeases God. The reason why all the Israelites who came out of Egypt except Joshua and Caleb perished in the wilderness was that they were reminiscent of the past. The priority in every trial is not to go back, but to find an opportunity for spiritual strengthening and purification by moving forward, confident in the divine plan. Let us tempt to put to death the old slavery to sin within us, that we may enjoy the freedom of God's promises in the kingdom of heaven. The desert is an inescapable and important stage in the life of the believer: we must cross the desert. In Christ there is no past, only future: "Therefore, if any man be in Christ, he is a new creature: old things are passed away; behold, all things are become new" (2 Corinthians 5:17). With Christ everything is advancement, conquest, and victory.

The journey through the desert leads to the Promised Land, but before entering it, we must cross the Jordan River. Joshua, trained in Moses's example to bring the challenges of leadership before Jehovah, instructed the people with Jehovah's instructions. Joshua received the mission ("Moses my servant is dead; now therefore arise, go over this Jordan, thou, and all this people, unto the land which I do give to them, even to the children of Israel" [Joshua 1:2]) and received confirmation ("Every place that the sole of your foot shall tread upon, that have I given unto you as I said unto Moses [Joshua 1:3])," and the victory was announced to him: "There shall not any man be able to stand before thee all the days of thy life: as I was with Moses, so I will be with thee: I will not fail thee, nor forsake thee" (Joshua 1:5). When God sends us and provides everything we need, we must simply act and trust him.

To begin, the Levitical priests would carry the ark of the covenant, and then, about two thousand cubits away, the people would follow them to know where they should cross. The humanly logical thing when you are going to cross a river is to look for a boat to sail across it, or to build a bridge to pass over the waters, or in the last case, to try to swim to the opposite shore. But God did not mention any of these methods, because he does not need human resources to perform miracles. Instead: "And Joshua said unto the people, Sanctify yourselves: for to morrow the Lord will do wonders among you" (Joshua 3:5). This was the pinnacle of forty years of purification through the wilderness: sanctification. Sanctify yourself today if you want to see miracles tomorrow. Holiness is the fertile ground wherein the power of God is formed. In the life of the believer, the Jordan is not a tourist attraction, it is a spiritual imperative. We all must cross our own Jordan to enter the Promised Land following the order established, with God marking the route and with the sanctified people following him. And when we are already in the Promised Land, enjoying the rest of the journey through the desert, let us raise an altar of worship to show gratitude, to worship, and to praise. The Promised Land is not for active sinners but for repentant and sanctified sinners. God takes us out of Egypt because he created us to be free and enjoy the wonders reserved in the Promised Land. Let us close our eyes and follow Jehovah confidently, for with him we will get to where we never thought we would be.

Because God is God, the Israelites entered Canaan, but now they had to own the land. It is not enough to arrive; you must stay. And for that, it is necessary to conquer. In God's work there is always room for development and growth. We can never do too much for God. The Spirit's work is finished when we are in his presence.

After crossing the river, the Israelites beheld the Jordan Valley before them, beautiful and splendid, but the city of Jericho stood in the way of their advance toward possessing the land. The news that Jehovah had separated the waters of the Jordan to allow the passage of the children of Israel had reached the ears of the inhabitants of Canaan quickly, and the kings of the area were fearful; their hearts fainted. The Bible says: "Now Jericho was straitly shut up because of the children of Israel: none went out, and none came in" (Joshua 6:1). It should be noted that the city was not closed because of the thieves who could steal, or the wild beasts that could devour them, but because of the children of Israel. The world system is totally closed to God to prevent him from entering, when the best option would be to include him, because in any case, no matter how much we oppose it, in the end the will of God will prevail. The requirement for taking a fortified city with strongly secured walls and gates is to have a trained army, the necessary weaponry, and the right strategy, but just like when crossing the Jordan, the instructions God gave Joshua were illogical. But even so, Joshua obeyed to the letter, because whenever we act by logic, we will obtain results, but if we act by faith, we will obtain miracles.

Jehovah gave his instructions beginning at the end, assuring them of victory: "And the Lord said unto Joshua, See, I have given into thine hand Jericho, and the king thereof, and the mighty men of valor" (Joshua 6:2). The normal thing is that the result of a battle is known when it ends, but when it is a battle of God, before starting we know that the victory is ours because he has given us the city. The second part of the instructions was no better: instead of attacking, he ordered not to attack. It is obvious that to take a city one must fight, but Jehovah said, "And ye shall compass the city, all ye men of war, and go round about the city once. Thus shalt thou do six days. And seven priests shall bear before the ark seven trumpets of rams horns: and the seventh day ye shall compass the city seven times, and the priest shall blow with the trumpets" (Joshua 6:3–4). We should note that God separated the walks around Jericho into two sections, the first being for six days, and last being on the seventh day. The number six is the number of men, which means that during the first six days the Israelites would surround the city in their limited humanity, and therefore the walls would not fall, but on the seventh day, seven priests with the seven horns would go around Jericho seven times. Seven is the number of God, and here we see three times seven, which represents the plenitude, perfection, and totality of God announced, proclaimed, and confirmed in the fulfillment of the divine mandate. At the end of the seventh lap, the horn had to sound for a long time and the people were to shout, and the city wall would fall. Exactly so, it happened. The taking of Jericho was not a military battle; it was a spiritual procession. The walls were torn down, surrounding the Israelites in worship, praise, prayer, and faith. The stage of the journey from Egypt to Canaan shows the way established by God to attain salvation: first, to come out of the slavery of sin and be regenerated by crossing the desert; second, to reach our Jordan River, where we have to sanctify ourselves to cross and enter the Promised Land; and third, to lead a life of spiritual procession, so that our cries may tear down the walls that prevent us from conquering what God has given us.

Joshua and the people of Israel who entered Canaan continued the conquest and division of the land until they fully possessed it as promised by Jehovah to Abraham, Isaac, and Jacob. God had fulfilled his promise and expected human beings to be faithful to their part of the covenant, namely, to show obedience and holiness.

God always exceeds humankind's expectations, but humankind always disappoints God's expectations.

The Wayward People (Judges)

As long as Joshua and the Israelites who conquered the Promised Land lived, the people remained faithful to Jehovah, but when they died, there was a leadership vacuum, and the Israelites rebelled by surrendering to the customs and religions of the peoples who lived in their surroundings. Jehovah's wrath fell upon them, and he delivered them into the hands of their enemies, who stole from them and frightened them, going so far as their having to live in caves to save their lives. This rebellion caused God to decide not to cast out of Canaan the nations that dwelt among them, to prove the lineage of Israel that knew no war. How is it possible that Jehovah's chosen, guided, and instructed people fell into such a low spiritual position? The answer is the same again: through their disobedience. To disobey God is to renounce all the privileges of his protection. God's rules are spears, and his counsels are a breastplate. Outside of God everything is chaos, confusion, loss, and defeat.

The book of Judges narrates this shameful and dark period of the history of the people of Israel. Again and again the same vicious cry was repeated: first, the Israelites disobeyed (as we have all done at some point), and as a consequence they fell into the hands of their enemies (in the same way that has happened to us), who stole the crops and plundered their cities. Then, in their despair, the Israelites cried out to Jehovah, and he raised up a leader to deliver them from aggressors (Judges 2:16), as he raised up one without equal for us, Jesus, who delivered us forever from disobedience and slavery, blessing us eternally with power over sin and blessing us totally. God will always raise up human beings with a special love for and devotion to his Word and his work to lead the people through adversities and bring them out of them. This spiritual cycle of rebellion, slavery, repentance, and salvation must happen in the life of a person, but it must not be repeated in the life of the believer.

In total, during the twenty-five hundred years covered by the book of Judges, from the death of Joshua until the time when the prophet Samuel anointed Saul as Israel's first king, twelve judges were raised up, men of arms who performed feats of faith to bring peace to the people during their period of leadership. But even so, the Israelites did not obey the judges and continued to worship other people's gods. Of these twelve judges, two of them, Gideon and Samson, not because they are the most famous, but because they were the only ones who received the ministering of the angel of Jehovah, which is the very presence of God, deserve special attention.

Thanks to the ministry of Deborah and Barak, the Israelites had enjoyed forty years of peace, but they disobeyed God again, as was their custom, and the cycle of human collapse and divine rescue began for the fifth time. On this occasion, for the past seven years, the Midianites and the Amalekites attacked the Israelites at harvesttime to steal all their food and leave them hungry. For this reason, the children of Israel had to cry out again to Jehovah, and Jehovah sent them a prophet who reminded them of all the things God had done for them. It is especially important to keep in mind all the blessings, all the aid, and all the solutions that God has given us, because the reasoning of faith is this: if God has blessed us up to this day, he will also bless us tomorrow. Based on what God has done in the past, we can trust God to come through for us in the future.

Gideon

Gideon was, in the inheritance of his father, Joash Abiezrite, in the practice of threshing wheat in the winepress to hide it from the Midianites. This was an act of cowardice, because usually the wheat was threshed in open places where the wind blew to separate the chaff, not in a sunken and closed place like a winepress, where the

Israelites crushed grapes for fermentation. Gideon worked secretly to prevent enemies from stealing the fruit of his sacrifice. Amid this anxiety came the angel of Jehovah, who is the same Spirit of Jesus ministering in the Old Testament: "And the angel of the Lord appeared unto him, and said unto him, The Lord is with thee, thou mighty man of valor" (Judges 6:12). This greeting was strange to Gideon, causing him to wonder, *Is Jehovah with me, and do the Midianites steal my harvest every year? Am I hardworking and courageous man, working in hiding because I have no courage to stand up for what I have achieved? Oh no, that greeting has nothing to do with me.* The believer has no reason to allow the enemy to steal his blessings, because "Jehovah is with us." The demoralization and loss of faith of the Israelites was so great that it was difficult for them to recognize themselves as God's people. There is nothing sadder and bleaker when, because of disobedience and sin, abandonment and hopelessness are the norms of life. Anyway, even though Gideon felt incapable and defeated, Jehovah said to him, "Go in this thy might" (Joshua 6:14). "This thy might" refers not to Gideon's muscular strength but to God's spiritual power. The Israelites with their strength had failed to overthrow the Midianites, but now Gideon, with this new strength, would be able to do so. There is no obstacle so great that it is impossible to overcome with the power of God. We must never live in the fear caused by the situation around us; we must reap the fruits of faith by confronting the enemy courageously, filled with the power of God.

The unbelief of human beings has always been proverbial, but God's patience is infinite. The very presence of Jehovah's angel was not enough to convince Gideon, so he asked for signs. The true believer lives by faith, and the trials will be seen in the vow of obedience. The proof he requested was intended to reveal the identity of the one he was talking about: was it human or divine? And it really consisted of something simple: *I beg you not to leave here until I come back to you and take out my offering and put it before you.* If Gideon, returning with the offering, which included a kid, of which he put the meat in a basket and the broth in a pot, and unleavened bread from an ephah of flour, by offering these things to the messenger, and if the messenger were to take it and nothing happened, it would be like a gift for a human, but if something supernatural were to happen when he presented his offering, then he would know he was in the presence of Jehovah. And this is exactly what happened. Upon receiving the offering, the angel of Jehovah stretched out his staff, touching the flesh and unleavened bread, and up blazed a fire that consumed everything, and amid the fire the angel of Jehovah disappeared. It was at that moment that Gideon became convinced that he had indeed been visited and commissioned by Jehovah to save the people of Israel.

Now it was up to Jehovah to test Gideon. That same night, Jehovah ordered him to build an altar to make a sacrifice of holocaust with a seven-year-old bull and to light the fire with the wood of the image of Baal. The bull was to be from Gideon's father's herd, which implies breaking with family authority, and the burning of the idols meant breaking with all kinds of spirituality alien to Jehovah. Before we begin the ministry of service to God, we must make disappear, in a sacrifice of renunciation, all human interests and all our spiritual inclinations that do not come from the throne of grace.

The slightest thing that separates us from God, we must burn it in the fire of the Holy Spirit. We must change our opinions and our beliefs to start from nothing on a new path to God, giving ourselves to him completely.

Gideon conducted the sacrifice but performed it at night out of fear for his family and his society. This is like going to church and hiding so no one knows you are there. Hiding one's faith does not please God. An eloquent example of the blessing of showing one's faith is seen in the prophet Daniel. When King Darius signed the edict forbidding petitions for thirty days to anyone but him, Daniel entered his own house, opened the windows of the room he was in, and knelt three times a day to pray to Jehovah with thanksgiving, challenging the human and social authority of King Darius in order to be faithful and obedient to Jehovah. For this reason, Daniel was thrown into the lions' den, but God rewarded his faithfulness by saving him from the jaws of the beasts. The fulfillment of a promise is not a gift, but a reward for our faithfulness. Daniel did not hide his face, and God protected him. We have countless powerful promises from God, but to receive and enjoy them, we must be faithful, consecrated, and obedient.

But even after Gideon had verified that Jehovah himself had appeared to him and commanded him to make a sacrifice where divine power was glorified, it was still not enough; he needed more signs to reaffirm his confidence. This act of asking God for proof had become a custom that denoted the spiritual decay of the Israelite people. Gideon tempted Jehovah twice by saying, "I will put a fleece of wool in the age, and if you make the fleece dawn full of dew and the land around dry, I will understand that you will save Israel by my hand." And God made it so. The first time was not enough, so now Gideon asked that it happen in the reverse way, that the fleece be dry and the dew be on the earth, and God again worked the miracle, not because of Gideon's demand, but to show his control over the elements of nature and provide the fulfillment of protection and salvation for God's people. However many obstacles he faced, it was not Gideon, who had God's help, but God, who did not have Gideon's confidence, who saved his people. Only Jehovah has the power to overcome this kind of war against such difficult enemies as doubt, fears, cowardice, and unbelief. That war was fought triumphantly by Jesus in the temptation of the desert, when Satan, with insane wickedness, proposed that he throw himself from the pinnacle of the temple, trusting in the promise that God would send his angels to hold him with his hands so that he would not stumble foot in stone. And the Son of God, in all the splendor of his divine strength, answered: "It is written again, thou shalt not tempt the Lord thy God" (Matthew 4:5–7).

Gideon had no spiritual discernment. Obedience is not based on signs; it must be based on faith.

The time of the harvest had come, and the Midianites and Amalekites, who together made an army much larger than that of the Israelites, had gathered to plunder Israel. Let us always keep in mind that when the harvest is ready, the enemy prepares to attack us and steal our blessing. Gideon took the people with him, thirty-two thousand men of war, to engage in battle and militarily defeat the enemy with his forces, but it would not happen exactly like this, as God had other plans. Jehovah ordered to decrease the number of Hebrew warriors. This was a test of obedience and faith, because from the beginning the Israelites were at a numerical disadvantage, so a decrease in the number of their soldiers would increase the enemy advantage, thereby increasing the chance of defeat, which was already high. But the battle, although it would take place on earth and would be fought between humans, would be fought by Jehovah, and he would obtain victory with miraculous actions, giving the victory to the people so that they would understand that without him, they would always be helpless, and therefore only obedience, worship, glorification, and honor of his name would set them free from oppression.

Deliverance comes from heaven, where our priest Jesus is seated at the right hand of the Father. No human victory has heavenly merit, only that achieved in the power of the Holy Spirit.

To make the first reduction, Jehovah sent Gideon to proclaim among the Israelites that the fearful could leave the camp. The next day, twenty thousand of them returned, leaving only one thousand. It seemed that it would be fine like this, but no, there were still many of them. For the second military decline, they were sent to the water to be evaluated there. One might think that God would organize a swimming competition, to choose the most athletic and resilient, but it was a challenge to quench thirst as they drank the water, to choose the most alert. Only and exclusively God's plans require such proof. The stranger it seems, the more it must come from God. "For who hath know the mind of the Lord? Or who hath been his counsellor?" (Romans 11:34)

The test was simple, just drinking water from a stream. Some would kneel to drink directly from the body of water, and others would stand cupping the water with their hands and bringing it to their mouths.

It happened that nine thousand seven hundred soldiers knelt, and three hundred remained on the spot. At the end, the three hundred who drank the water by bringing it to their mouths with their hands, keeping their eyes on the surroundings so as not to be surprised, were the ones chosen to bring about the salvation of God's people. Being spiritually alert prevents sin, secures victory, and provides salvation. Circumstances can lead us through strange and inexplicable facts, and we must look for the reasons and motives to find the consequences. It is essential to win battles if we are to have biblical perspective, divine intuition, and spiritual sense.

God defeated the Midianites by having them withdraw using a dream, which was interpreted as the invincible superiority of God's people. Gideon then confronted and pursued the Midianite army and eliminated its kings and princes until completely subjugating them. To achieve victory, the children of Israel proposed that Gideon rule over them, but he refused, saying that it would be Jehovah who would reign, a very correct determination on his part. In return he asked for all the golden earrings that they had, a very unfortunate decision, with which he made a golden ephod (superior priestly garment), which then diverted the people into idolatry. Biblically it cannot be determined why he did this, but we can assume that it was to have a reminder of the deliverance that God had given them on that day. Still, without intending to do so, he created an idol. The second commandment says, "Thou shalt not make unto thee any graven image, or any likeness of any thing that is in heaven above, or that is in the earth beneath, or that is in the water under the earth" (Exodus 20:4), and surely, Gideon knew this commandment. Despite his doubts and mistakes, Jehovah provided Gideon with the ability to bring peace to Israel during the forty years he lived after these events, but when he died, the children of Israel again prostituted themselves by going after Baal.

Samson

The same intervention of Jehovah's angel that Gideon experienced is the one we see here now ministering the birth of Samson, to dedicate him to the same ministry, that is, saving God's people. A similar peculiarity between the two men is that just as Gideon was threshing the wheat hidden in a winepress for fear of the Midianites and showed no interest in the deliverance of Israel, the wife of Manoah, mother of Samson, despite being barren, was not praying for the blessing of a son, let alone a son who would save God's people from the oppression of the Philistines.

While human beings remain busy providing for their human appetites and ignoring their spiritual needs, God always finds an opportunity to spring into action with the initiative of salvation. When incipient humanity was lost in hopeless sin, Jehovah gave birth to Israel as a holy nation to establish his covenant of salvation with humankind through them, now choosing Samson before he was conceived and setting him apart as a Nazarite for the salvation of the nation of Israel. Genesis 1:1 says, "In the beginning God created the heavens and the earth," which means that our God is the God of principles, who is always in the beginning, and from him comes all the beginnings. Nothing can begin first without God, because, in the beginning, God created, is creating, and will create all things. Knowing this, let us all begin our projects by placing God "in the beginning."

The first instructions of obedience and holiness were given to Samson's future mother: "Now therefore beware, I pray thee, and drink not wine nor strong drink, and eat not any unclean thing" (Judges 13:4). How important is a family given to the Lord! The family is the human nucleus created and designed by God to preserve Christian ethical and moral values within society. This is the true meaning of "you are the salt of the earth" (Matthew 5:13). When the family breaks down, spiritual cohesion disappears. Human conglomerates need preestablished codes of conduct that define the discipline and valuation of individual acts as active factors in influencing the results of the collective. This is what we call the legal constitution of an established social entity, be it a country, an institution, or an organization. To this day, the most just and equitable legal constitutions are those that follow God's merciful pattern of justice embodied in the Bible. The greater the society's closeness to God, the greater the social justice.

Manoah watched his wife approach him, excited by the news that an angel had told him he would have a child. Nothing makes a woman happier than knowing that she is going to be a mother. Many women do not know it, but being a mother, in addition to being a blessing, is a fulfillment of God's plan for the continuation of life. Motherhood, along with fatherhood, is the component of God's call to "bear fruit and multiply" given to Adam at creation. Perhaps, noting the surprising nature of this event, Manoah was not completely convinced, and wanted to talk to the angel to check if everything were true. So he prayed to Jehovah to resend the angel and asked him what they should do with the child who would be born. When the man (Jehovah's angel) returned and stood before Manoah, Manoah asked him, "Are you that man who spoke to the woman?" And the man answered, "I am" (Judges 13:11). This is a clear indication of Jesus's preexistence and his ministering in the Old Testament. Manoah's request was heeded and answered, not precisely to please him, but to reassure him that they should do what had already been told to his wife. When God answers our requests, it is an exhortation to obey what is already written in the Bible.

What happens next in the story deserves special attention because of the revelation it implies. Manoah wanted to thank Jehovah for the deference he had received, so he asked the man to stay and offered him a goat, not in sacrifice to God, but as food, for he thought he was talking to a man, probably a prophet. But the answer changes the meaning of the text from earthly to heavenly: "And the angel of the Lord said unto him, Though thou detain me, I will not eat of thy bread" (the human and spiritual points of view are very different). He added: "And if thou wilt offer a burnt offering [sacrifice to God that included burning the offering after it was sacrificed], thou must offer it unto the Lord" (Judges 13:16), giving a veiled reference to his identity. But Manoah still did not understand the supernatural nature of what was happening, and he asked, insisting on human gratitude, without realizing that what was imperative was the worship of God, "What is thy name, that when thy sayings come to pass we may do thee honor? And the angel of the Lord said unto him, Why asked thou thus after my name, seeing it is secret?" (Judges 13:17–18). From beginning to end, the Bible speaks of Jesus. The Old Testament is the annunciation; the Gospels, the confirmation; the New Testament letters, the explanation; and Revelation, the manifestation. Anyway, "Manoah took a kid with a meat offering, and offered it upon a rock unto the Lord: and the angel did wondrously; and Manoah and his wife looked on. For it came to pass, when the flame went up toward heaven from the altar, that the angel of the Lord ascended in the flame of the altar. And Manoah and his wife looked on it, and fell on their faces to the ground" (Judges 13:19–20).

When Abraham was willing to sacrifice his son Isaac to Jehovah, the miracle of the provision of the ram happened. When the Israelites made a sacrifice of holiness to Jehovah, the miracle of the separation of the waters of the Jordan to enter the Promised Land happened. When God's people made a spiritual procession sacrifice for seven days around Jericho, its walls fell. Whenever we make a sacrifice of praise, worship, obedience, and holiness to Jehovah, miracles will occur. That was what happened here.

Jehovah was not in the fire, nor did he go with the fire. Jehovah uses fire as an element within his plans to fulfill his purposes. Thus, he appeared to Moses in the burning bush to call him and commission him to free God's people from slavery in Egypt, because God is the owner of the fire. Nothing escapes the power of God.

After all this, Samson was born and raised with God's blessing, and the Spirit of Jehovah was manifested upon him. Samson had the privilege of being chosen, even before being conceived in his mother's womb, to fulfill a special purpose of God. But, and this is a sad human *but*, he did not know how to value the transcendence of his mission. He possessed enormous human strength, but he was totally weak spiritually, and yet he had all the necessary potential given directly by God to perform the great feats required to overcome the Philistines, which he did because of the conflicts he had created by, because of his disobedience, marrying and relating to Israel's enemies—and not with the express intention of fulfilling God's plan of deliverance for his people. And although the Bible says that Samson judged Israel for twenty years, he did so by his own lusts and not by his obedience to God. Samson was a failure, but in the great mercy and immense divine grace extended upon human beings as a protective mantle, he was allowed to serve to facilitate Jehovah's will. Even rebels are used to promote God's plans.

Samuel: Israel's Sociopolitical Change

The spiritual decay of the people of Israel was at its lowest, to such an extent that, the Bible says, "In those days there was no king in Israel; but every man did that which was right in his own eyes" (Judges 17:6). In other words, the sociopolitical situation of the Israelites was one of chaos. This disorder led to their dependence on the nations that dwelt around them. The cycle of sin, servitude, supplication, and salvation, which had been repeated countless times, was leading the people to total separation from God, and it was necessary to break this disorderly pattern of conduct, updating the system of social and political direction, because the method of government through judges did not work. The human being, by himself, is incapable of properly conducting himself spiritually. He needs the direct guidance of God through the presence of the Holy Spirit within his life, controlling all its aspects and facets. After three hundred years of setbacks, an update on government was imposed.

Although God can do his work by himself, he has given us the high honor of placing into our hands that wonderful task, using people ready to serve whom he chooses from before birth. He calls them during their daily lives to direct them through tough times and strategic places. The prophet Samuel was one of those so called, being used as a bridge between the abyss left by the judges and the stage of the kings. Even Samuel's sons, Joel and Abijah, when they became judges, did not walk in their father's ways, so the elders of Israel gathered to make a king to unite them and judge them, as Samuel had grown old and was unfit to do the work. Samuel anointed two kings, one of the men, Saul, and another of God, David. Saul started out well but ended badly. David started out badly but ended well.

The stage of kings gave Israel a political and social cohesion as a nation that they had lost while they were only twelve tribes united by a law they did not respect, but the spiritual situation during this stage of reigns, which lasted four hundred fifty years, did not change for the better; basically, apostasy, idolatry, and disobedience to God were maintained throughout the stage of kings. The first three of them, Saul, David, and Solomon, with ups and downs, managed to keep the kingdom united for one hundred twenty years, but when Solomon died, the decision that his son Rehoboam made about the Israelites when he ascended the throne displeased the people, causing ten of the tribes of Israel to separate, led by Jeroboam, constituting the kingdom of Israel or the Northern Kingdom, and settle in the city of Samaria, while the other two tribes, of Judah and Benjamin, remained in Jerusalem faithful to Rehoboam, forming the Southern Kingdom or kingdom of Judah. Thus began the division of the Israelite nation and the enmity between the Jews and Samaritans, despite their belonging to the same people of God.

The Prophets: Attempt at Reconciliation

The first mention of the word *prophet* in the Bible is found in Genesis 20:7, referring to Abraham, when he descended to Gerar after the destruction of Sodom and Gomorrah, during the events between him and Abimelech because of Sarah, Abraham's wife. Later, the word *prophet* was attributed to Aaron, before going to Egypt with his brother, Moses, and appearing before Pharaoh (Exodus 7:1). During the biblical narrative, many other people were called prophets, God's representatives before humankind. Prophetic ministry was the first spiritual office until Jehovah instituted Aaron and his sons as priests of the tabernacle. Men called to be prophets, based on Jehovah's Word written in the law, made judgments about the people of Israel by showing them their disobedience and announcing the consequences that this would bring them. Although prophecy includes announcing events that would occur in the future, such as prophecies about the Messiah to come, and revelations of dream visions or interpretations, or those related to the end times in Revelation, it is wrong to confuse all the prophecies as predictions. Prophesying is talking about what is known by study, by experience, or by deduction, and in certain cases by divine revelation. The prophets knew the law because they had studied it, and they knew the disobedience of the people by experience, and from there they issued a judgment by deduction.

A simple example of this from everyday life is when we meet a couple who frequently get into intense arguments and say, any time a misfortune occurs, "This is what happens." In this case, they have only made a rational deduction based on the elements of judgment that they know. That is Bible prophecy. Now, God can, and indeed does, reveal to us situations that are to happen later in time, to warn us of danger, direct our ministry and spiritual life, or confirm his will in what we are doing for him. Something also important to know is that all prophecy related to God is based on the Bible and is about the church, and its main goal is to build up the body of Christ. In addition, exaggerating the use and extent of prophecy is dangerous because, in doing so, we may be found operating in a spirit of divination, which is condemned by God (Deuteronomy 18:9–12; Leviticus 19:26–31).

From their beginnings, the prophets conducted the tireless work of exhortation and defense of God and his written Word, beseeching the people to turn away from idols and turn to Jehovah. The prophets assisted, admonished, and guided the kings, some with good intentions, some with bad intentions, but all their acts, counsel, and revelations served Jehovah's purposes. They tried to bring God's people into God's good graces, to provoke an encounter between them, to lead them on paths of peace and blessing in obedience and holiness. All the prophets died conducting their ministries. Jehovah brought them out of nowhere; they were heroes, and they became martyrs. Something common to all of them was that before God called them, they had no hope, but after responding to the voice of the Creator, they entered the glory of heaven. Sufferings and pains can kill the body but not the spirit. The prophets understood it that way and resisted to the end, pursuing the supreme prize, the salvation of the soul. "But he that shall endure unto the end, the same shall be saved" (Matthew 24:13).

Malachi: The Break

All human beings called by God to serve in the reconquest of holiness by obedience to his Word based on faith and love, in one way or another, to a greater or lesser degree, intentionally or unintentionally, had failed him. Something innate in human beings prevented them from reaching the necessary level of spirituality required to satisfy the holiness of God, their having inherited the sinful nature from Adam and Eve. A solution had to be found to repair this defect. The situation was not that God had had too much of human disobedience; it was that humankind had received much from God, his love, his compassion, and his forgiveness. Rebellious Israel, wayward and disrespectful, had to be put in their place and face the consequences of their evil attitudes, for they had already been rescued countless times from the disasters of their misfortunes and had made the same mistakes repeatedly.

The book of the prophet Malachi reflects Jehovah's spiritual mood in relation to the Israelites. God begins by declaring that he had loved the Israelites and chosen them, establishing his right to be obeyed (Malachi 1:2); continues to reproach them for their dishonesty and fear (Malachi 1:6); pronounces to the priests the instructions to achieve reconciliation (Malachi 2:2); announces that there will be a judgment upon them (Malachi 3:5); and says at the end, despite all that has happened, that he will leave open the door to hope (Malachi 4:2). Malachi, from the beginning, makes it clear that what will be said is against the people of Israel (Malachi 1:1), marking a breaking point due to the discrepancies of views. "God said to them, I have loved you, and they answered, In what did you love us?" (Malachi 1:2); "God said, You despise my name, and they answered him, In what case have we despised your name?" (Malachi 1:6); "God said, You offered unclean bread on my altar thinking that the table of Jehovah is despicable, and you said, In what case have we dishonored you?" (Malachi 1:7); "You have made Jehovah weary with your words, and you say, How have we tired him?" (Malachi 2:17); "Return to me, and I will turn to you, said the Lord of hosts. But you said, What are we to become?" (Malachi 3:7); God said, You have stolen from me. And you said, What have we stolen from you?" (Malachi 3:8); "Your words against me have been violent, says Jehovah. And you said, What have we spoken against you?" (Malachi 3:13). The insolence of the nation of Israel had reached an intolerable limit. The Israelites had turned away from Jehovah and turned the law into a social custom, setting aside the spiritual principle of it, loving God because he loved them first, and doing so with all their hearts, and with all their souls, and with all their minds. The Israelites offered unclean bread and defective animals to Jehovah, things clearly forbidden in Leviticus 22:20–23 and Deuteronomy 15:21, so he said to them, "I have no pleasure in you, … neither will I accept an offering at your hand" (Malachi 1:10).

The rebuke goes on to remind the priests that Jehovah had made a covenant with Levi of life and peace that he would be afraid of God, and he had humbled himself and had taught the law with truth, and many had turned away from evil because the priest had the responsibility to keep wisdom, for he was Jehovah's messenger of hosts. But the priests of Malachi's time had departed from the law, perverted the sacrifices, and discredited the priesthood, and therefore God made them vile and low before the people.

These were sad and desolate times for Jehovah's people because of their folly and inclination to sin. God suffered for this reason. There is no greater pain for a father than to see his children lost, poor, and desperate. But in the suffering of a father is born the hope of the children. God's immense love for his people created the way back to him, guided by the messenger he would send to appear in the temple as Lord and angel of the covenant. Since Jehovah does not change no matter how serious the faults committed, we have not been consumed. Jehovah's people had turned their backs on the temple obligations by failing to deliver tithes and offerings. God is not so much concerned with courage as he is concerned with action. It is not a question of what needs to be given, but one of understanding the need to participate. The Israelites had diverted their attention from God's laws; therein lay the fact of theft, in the absence of dedication, negligence in the fulfillment, and forgetfulness of the relationship. Returning to the temple bringing tithes meant obedience, humiliation, thanksgiving, interest, and responsibility. "Bring ye all the tithes into the storehouse, that there may be meat in mine house, and prove me now herewith, saith the Lord of hosts, if I will not open you the windows of heaven, and pour you out a blessing, that there shall not be room enough to receive it" (Malachi 3:10).

Salvation always comes from Jehovah. So, God had even more;

he is an inexhaustible source of grace and mercy, anointing us with peace, love, and security. God promises a severe judgment of fire on the proud, "but for the humble, those who fear him, obey his Word, and worship his name, the Son of righteousness will be born, the truth of God illuminating their lives, and in his wings he will bring salvation, and you will go free to enjoy his freedom; you will jump strong and prosperous in the Lord, and you will tread down the wicked, enjoying the victory of the Lord" (Malachi 4:1–3). Jehovah's reproaches and scolding are to cleanse impurities, remove obstacles, and bring us to a new stage that far surpasses the ones of the past. The book of the prophet Malachi marks the end of a path that led nowhere, to make room for a wide avenue that would reach the throne of grace. The time and the seasons had come for true repentance and the great harvest. Holiness was back at the gates; you could smell the aroma of God's purity floating over a lost and wayward humanity, which could not straighten out its steps toward salvation.

CHAPTER 6

THE FULFILLMENT OF TIME

Jehovah withdrew from the spiritual life of the people of Israel for four hundred years. Time relieves the pain of unavoidable wounds but sharpens the suffering of those wounds caused by negligence, carelessness, or disinterest. This was the situation between Jehovah and Israel. The Israelites suffered because of their rebellion. God had not made any mistake that he had to rectify. He had known from the beginning that this would happen, and he was aware and waiting for the moment to solve human spiritual insufficiency, which was not a learned attitude but an acquired inheritance. What was going to happen was not a plan B, because God does not need second choices, or back doors, or secret passages. What would happen was destined to happen since before the foundation of the world. Four centuries had passed since Malachi's ministry, and despite the many generations of Israelites that had passed, they did not return to God's love. The priests did not restore the spirituality of the law, and the people continued to offer imperfect sacrifices on the altar of Jehovah, forgetting to bring tithes and offerings to the temple. Therefore, judgment remained upon the people.

God had previously intervened in human history during the time of Noah, when he sent rains for forty days and caused a flood that cleansed the earth of the wickedness that humankind had incurred, saving only Noah, a man of faith, but one polluted with sin, and his family. Now God would intervene a second time, in a unique way, sending a man filled with the power of the Holy Spirit and uncontaminated with sin, who would flood the earth with holiness to save humankind.

The fulfillment of the time mentioned in Galatians 4:4 had come. This moment is closely related to the predictive prophecy of Genesis 3:15, which announces, "And I will put enmity between you and the woman, and between thy seed and her seed; it shall bruise thy head, and thou shalt bruise his heel." According to our modern idiosyncrasy, except the announcement of a Savior, there is nothing that attracts attention in this prophecy, because in our days, fatherhood and motherhood are at the same level in the procreation of children, but for the patriarchal societies of that time, where family descent was counted following the paternal line, this statement about the seed of the woman made it something unusual. The purpose was to make a distinction for what would be the last Adam. The first Adam came from dust, and to dust returned, where he disappeared, whereas the last Adam came from God, and to God he returned, where he remains forever. "And no man hath ascended up to heaven, but he that came down from heaven, even the Son of man which is in heaven" (John 3:13). The first Adam offended God, whereas we can ask the last Adam for forgiveness. The first Adam introduced sin into humankind, whereas the last Adam delivers humankind of sin. God made the first man Adam a living soul; the last Adam, life-giving Spirit. The plan of salvation came from the moment the first sin was committed and was fulfilled in the sufficient and eternal sacrifice of the last Adam: "Neither is there salvation in any other: for there is none other name under heaven given among men, whereby we must be saved" (Acts 4:12). Until now, the law of Moses, established on spiritual principles to maintain the identity and national unity of the Hebrew people, had remained on an intellectual level, to be known and applied, but the Israelites had made it optional with respect to obedience, setting aside the covenant established with Jehovah at Mount Sinai. This time it would be different: God's law would enter our minds and be written in our hearts, so that we could truly be his people and he could truly be our God. Obviously, another man could not come from human reproduction, that is, copulation between a man and a woman, because in this way that man would be a person contaminated with sinful inheritance and everything would continue in the same vein. To achieve this goal, it was necessary to re-create a human being with DNA free from the defect of sin.

God is not repetitive, but creative, and therefore he would not create another human being from the dust of the earth. Now it would be something much more authentic, more direct from God, involving him directly, by incarnating in the form of a human being, but without sin, living among sinners, but without sin, so that sinful human beings might live as holy human beings—the supreme humiliation and, at the same time, the subtlest exaltation (Philippians 2:5–11).

The Miracle

During this time, surely, in Jerusalem lived many young women and virgins consecrated to Jehovah, with sufficient spiritual condition to be chosen and be part of God's definitive plan of salvation for humanity, but only one could be selected, because there would be only one Messiah. The Bible says in Luke 1:28: "And the angel came in unto her, and said, Hail, thou that art highly favored; the Lord is with thee: blessed art thou among women." The expression that the angel used when addressing Mary deserves special attention: blessed are you *among* women, not *above* women. Mary was not better than the others, nor was she above them, nor is it implied that because of her being chosen for this unique mission, she was to be considered superior or worthy of some special worship. She would continue to be a woman equal to the others, but with a different task.

She still did not come out of her amazement, and the angel continued to announce to her that she would conceive in her womb and have a son who would be called Jesus, who was to be great, called the Son of the Highest, and to whom would be given the throne of David his father to reign over the house of Jacob forever (Luke 1:30–33). Even more astonishing, "Then said Mary unto the angel, How shall this be, seeing I know not a man?" (Luke 1:35). This is a common situation for spiritual miracles. We are worried, as Mary was, about how this would happen because we do not focus on *who* is going to do it. An analogous situation is found in Acts 12:4–16, when the apostle Peter was imprisoned for his preaching of the gospel, and the church prayed unceasingly to God for him. In response to this fervent prayer of the church, an angel of the Lord appeared and woke Peter to get him out of prison. At that moment the chains fell off his hands and the angel was in front of him, and he kept thinking it was a vision. So the guards passed and the exit door was opened to reach the street, and then the angel left him. Peter went to the house where the brothers were praying for his release, and when he knocked on the door, they thought it was the angel (to tell them that he had died), and he had to insist that they open the door for him. When they saw him, they were stunned. If they were praying to God to set Peter free, why, when he was released, were they unable to believe it? We pray to God constantly about the various difficulties that arise in our lives, and when God answers our prayers, we often resist believing it, or give the situation a human answer.

The miracle of Mary's pregnancy consisted in the act of conception, where no man intervened, but the Holy Spirit and the power of the Highest. After the miraculous virginal conception, the nine months of gestation passed naturally, with the discomforts of the process. And the birth, which was also virginal, because she "did not know a man," happened the same as everyone's, with pushes and pains. And of course, during childbirth she lost her virginity. This event, unique in history, of the union of the Holy Spirit and human flesh in Mary's womb is theologically known as "the hypostatic union." It was in Jesus that for the first time the Holy Spirit lived internally within a person along with the flesh.

During the Old Testament, Jehovah's Spirit never ministered like the Holy Spirit. At this stage, God sent his Spirit upon chosen servants to train, guide, and strengthen them in such a way that they would be able to accomplish the task entrusted to them, but he had never dwelt within them to fill them in the manner that he did with Jesus and as he does today with us. None of the men of the Old Testament enjoyed the indwelling and fullness of the Holy Spirit in their lives. This is a privilege unique to believers after the ministry of Christ. God's plans have a primary characteristic shown throughout the Bible, and that is that everything is prepared in advance. God's miracles are not hasty actions performed at the last hour to overcome unexpected obstacles. The Bible declares that the entire process of Jesus's incarnation as Savior of the World was prepared and destined from before the foundation of the world. God became human in Jesus Christ at the exact moment to change the spiritual configuration of human beings. The fact of the all-powerful holy God turned into a human being is a concept that has always been under discussion, and has been misunderstood and tergiversated, creating much confusion, because it has been interpreted that in Jesus live two different people within the same individual, which is not the case.

The first man was created from the dust of the earth, in other words, personal creation from natural creation, and it failed. This time it would be a man created of the same essence and divine nature, avoiding any intervention outside of holiness; "therefore also that holy thing which shall be born of thee shall be called the Son of God" (Luke 1:35). For God to become 100 percent man, he had to be born of a woman, but because no male factor intervened in his conception, he retained 100 percent of the Divinity, without contamination of the sinful inheritance. In this way, Jesus was 100 percent man and 100 percent God, because in him the two natures harmoniously cohabit, forming a personality. This is the way to understand the humanity and divinity of Jesus, two natures united in one personality. The precise illustration of this is our composition. No one is 50 percent of his father and 50 percent of his mother, but our DNA is composed of 100 percent of our father's hereditary factors and 100 percent of our mother's hereditary factors, resulting not in 200 percent, but in the 100 percent of our unique individuality.

Adam's carnality was manifested when the first temptation came. It was now necessary to tempt Jesus to show the world that he was incapable of sinning because of his divine nature. Jesus was called to guide and teach by example. When John the Baptist began his ministry, baptizing the people in the Jordan River for the forgiveness of sins, Jesus went to him to be baptized, and although John objected, Jesus insisted, saying, "Suffer it to be so now: for thus is becometh us to fulfill all righteousness" (Matthew 3:13–17). He was setting an example of humility and obedience, showing that there is an order to maintain and rules to follow, and when we do so, the Holy Spirit comes to live in us in a notorious way, so that we can resist the temptations that are sure to come. Followed by his baptism and anointing, "then was Jesus led up of the Spirit into the wilderness, to be tempted of the devil" (Matthew 4:1). Temptations are allowed as trials and exercises of spiritual growth. If God allowed his Son Jesus to be tempted, why can't we be tempted?

After forty days of fasting and prayer in the wilderness, Satan tempted Jesus in the very areas in which he had succeeded in deceiving Eve: the lust of the flesh, the lust of the eyes, and the pride of life. Satan said to Eve: "Hath God said ye shall not eat of every tree of the garden [the lust of the flesh]? For God doth know that in the day ye eat thereof, then your eyes shall be opened [the lust of the eyes], and ye shall be as gods, knowing good and evil [the pride of life]" (Genesis 3:5). Eve let herself be involved in the diabolical scheme and fell into the trap because she trusted herself, but with Jesus it happened completely differently. Satan said to him, "If you are the Son of God, say that these stones should become bread [the lust of the flesh]." He continued with: "If you are the Son of God, cast yourself down; for it is written: To his angels he will command over you, and, in his hands they will sustain you, that he may not stumble upon your foot in stone [the pride of life]," the scene finishing with, "He took him to the pinnacle of the temple and showed him all the kingdoms of the world and the glory of them and said to him, All this I will give you, if prostrate you worship me [the lust of the eyes]" (Matthew 4:3–10). Jesus subjected his human nature to the power of divinity and rejected the satanic attack, defending his holiness using the Word of God.

Jesus taught us that by taking refuge in God's instructions, we will overcome the temptations of the devil, because the way to achieve total victory over Satan is through holiness. After Jesus defeated temptation, he began his ministry. To do God's work, one must first be baptized into repentance for the forgiveness of one's sins, then be anointed by the Spirit, then demonstrate that anointing by resisting temptations and overcoming trials. "Blessed is the man who endures temptation; for when he has withstood the test, he will receive the crown of life, which God has promised to those who love him" (James 1:12).

But we know that we cannot be like Jesus because we are sinners and Jesus never knew sin. The apostle James tells us, "For whosoever shall keep the whole law, and yet offend in one point, he is guilty of all" (James 2:10). This means that Christianity is a hundred-point exam, and the only possible way to pass is to get those hundred points. So, what can we do? Because the level of spirituality required to pass the test is humanly impossible to attain, we depend on the kindness of the Teacher. The points that we may miss, he can award to us based on our effort and sacrifice in trying to reach the highest possible score. This is how God's grace works. We are separated from him because of sin, and we can do nothing to fix it, only consecrate ourselves to Jesus to grant us the forgiveness and holiness necessary to pass the examination of salvation.

The Return to God

In the physical life, to return is to return to a previous position located somewhere or sometime in the past, but in the Christian faith (spiritual life), to return to God is to advance to the future that Jesus has prepared. Usually, returns begin where we are, but the return to God begins in the place where we accept Jesus Christ and ends when we are in the presence of God. Realizing that the position in which we find ourselves does not provide that which is necessary to realize ourselves as individuals, due to a deficit of spirituality, leads us to search for better locations to establish ourselves, looking for a specific objective, deciphering the failed interiority that overwhelms us, where the only way we can find the answers to our reality is to seek Jesus, the perfect model of being human. Everything we want to be is Jesus, so being like him is the best way for us to be. The first human identity was Adam, but in him we lost holiness and were separated from God. Now, our identity can only be recovered in Jesus.

But we must realize that Jesus Christ is not found in the past, but in the present and extending to eternal life. Before surrendering ourselves to Jesus, we live in a state of spiritual degeneration because of the sin that corrodes and destroys our relationship with God, but from the wonderful moment that we accept him as Lord and personal Savior, the Holy Spirit begins the process of regeneration, which only God is able to realize because, on the natural plane, when something degenerates and loses its physical and organic properties, there is no system or method to return to it the characteristics that it previously possessed. Regeneration is a miracle operated on the believer by faith in Jesus and the power of the Holy Spirit. God is the only One who can turn the bad into good and the rotten into new. That is the reason spiritual regeneration is not merely optional; it is the only option. As we remove what displeases God in our lives, the empty spaces are filled by holiness.

The processes, of whatever kind they may be, have a specific order established to achieve their objectives in the most effective way possible, but regeneration is aimed at creating a new nature that reinstalls the lost sanctity and achieves the reconstruction of the spiritual structure of the human being, cleansing the person of contamination of sin to restore him or her to his or her original condition, as God created the person to be. This restoration happens by renouncing the past, surrendering to a present of faith and obedience, and appropriating the future in the security of salvation and eternal life.

The first step in this process of drawing closer to God is repentance. To repent is not to feel remorse for what we have done; it is to reject and repudiate the sin that separates us and damages our relationship with him. When we repent, we ask God for forgiveness, and this act commutes the penalty we deserve to suffer for our sins. We receive forgiveness by confessing that the sacrifice of Jesus on the cross, as the fulfillment of our sins, releases us from condemnation. This is the effect of redemption. We must differentiate between redemption and rescue to appreciate the value and dimension of Jesus's sacrifice. If, when a person is taken captive, to free him we organize a special command, and through armed action he is taken out of captivity, it is a ransom, but when we use a mediator to establish a price for the release of the captive and we pay that price to free him, it is redemption. That is what Jesus did: he paid for our deliverance from the power of sin because we were captive. Jesus redeemed us; he is our Redeemer.

After repenting in exchange for faith in the eternal and sufficient sacrifice Jesus made on the cross of Calvary, and despite having been forgiven, for which we will not suffer the punishment we deserve, we are still guilty, and therefore something else must happen to acquit us. This is when justification is required, to exonerate us of guilt. God understands that our innate inclination to disobedience is due to the sinful inheritance derived from Adam and that no human being has had the option to choose his or her spiritual nature at birth, meaning that we did not choose to be sinners but we inherited sin, and no one is guilty. What we have inherited is why God justifies us, attributing the guilt of our sins to the one who really caused them, Satan. The Bible says: "Come now, and let us reason together, saith the Lord: though your sins be as scarlet, they shall be as white as snow; though they be red like crimson, they shall be as wool" (Isaiah 1:18).

Following repentance, forgiveness, and justification, we are ready for new birth, adoption, and holiness. The new birth introduces us to a supernatural spiritual dimension, which transforms our natural human condition into a new life. Because of the change of goals, we begin to pursue to please and honor God. The consolidation of this new life puts us in a position to be adopted as children of God. Here we must highlight some details related to adoption. First, God does not need to adopt us, because he already has a child. Second, when someone goes to adopt a child, they look for children with a good history, which none of us have. Third, why didn't God adopt obedient angels instead of disobedient human beings? This question shows us the immense privilege we have of being made children of God by adoption and, therefore, brothers of Jesus Christ. Brotherhood with Jesus is spiritual and bloody. It is spiritual by faith, and bloody by the blood shed on the cross. And fourth, adopted children have the same legal rights as natural children. This makes us heirs together with Christ, giving us the right to salvation from the throne of grace. Being adopted places us under God's authority (his Word) and protection (the power of the Holy Spirit). Authority and protection work together; obeying God's authority activates spiritual protection. There is no greater and more wonderful work than that which God has done for humankind. If in any way in human words I were to seek to describe it, I would call it God's infinity creativity capacity. In each next step comes a new connection, transmission, and conclusion.

All children need a father to guide and protect them, and our new heavenly Father covers and secures all spheres of our activity. We, after so long having been captives of sin, when Jesus frees us, have no home and do not know where to go, so God offers us his house (the church), to be welcomed into a family where we are guided and enabled to begin a new life. The relationship established with divinity through this fatherhood is wonderful. God the Son leads us to know God the Father, so that God the Holy Spirit may dwell in us and elevate us to the rank of children of God along with Jesus.

In Luke 12:32 Jesus said: "Fear not, little flock; for it is your Father's good pleasure to give you the kingdom." Human society is governed by its institutions, but eternal destinies are controlled by God, and that includes the world's system. God knew that satanic strategies with their false religions, atheism or liberalism, were going to separate most people from the truth and that those of us who would follow his Word would always be few, but he assures us that this does not mean that we are less because he is less, because he is and we, and we make a majority. The world hallucinates with houses, cars, and money, which enslave and do not last forever, but God, with all pleasure and joy, grants us a kingdom that liberates eternally. The new adoption we now enjoy makes us heirs to the greatest treasure, the kingdom of God in heaven.

To enjoy all the benefits of fatherhood and divine inheritance, we must fulfill the duties of consecrated and obedient children, and this exemplary behavior required before God is called holiness. No one can be perfect, but we can, as humanly as us possible, reach a spiritual level of excellence. If we can live in holiness, let us simply turn away from the sin that displeases God and separates us from him. To be holy is not to become the Invisible Man or to fly like ghosts in the movies. To be holy is to act in complete obedience to the Word of God and subject ourselves to the authority of the Holy Spirit. Holiness needs to be regained because it was the initial condition in which God created Adam, and because of his disobedience he lost it and was cast out of the garden. Therefore, to return to the presence of God, we must appropriate lost holiness by being obedient. To be holy is a divine command: "Because it is written, Be ye holy; for I am holy" (1 Peter 1:16). Holiness is not an abstract concept inapplicable to the daily life of faith; on the contrary, it is very useful and real in the spiritual growth and development of the believer, because the essence of the manifestation of sin is a bad attitude, an evil condition of the heart that leads a person to disobey God. Because of this, it seems to us that sin is not so harmful, but something slight that does not bother. But by confronting sin with holiness, we identify the demonic provenance in the nature of these actions and are able to reject them.

The fact of being holy is not an esoteric category that one acquires after death. It is a spiritual quality that transforms us into a unique class during life, children of God. From the moment of the consecration of our lives to Jesus Christ as our Savior, we begin to act biblically in all the circumstances and moments of our lives, and that difference marks our lives in relation to humankind and separates us before God. Moreover, as the central law of the gospel, holiness holds every human being accountable to divine judgment, because being holy is an aspect not just of what we should be but also of all that we must be.

Holiness Brought from Heaven to Earth

In Isaiah 6:1–3 the prophet narrates his visual experience of the Lord (Jesus, according to John 12:39–41) sitting on his high throne (because he is superior), sublime (because he is exalted), surrounded by seraphim, angels destined for the exaltation and worship of God: "And one cried unto another, and said, Holy, holy, holy, is the Lord of hosts: the whole earth is full of his glory" (Isaiah 6:3). The triple mention of the word *holy* serves as an affirmation, confirmation, and ratification of the incomparable holiness of God, as well as being a reference to the Most Holy Trinity, Holy Father, Holy Son, and Holy Spirit. The Bible declares in Hebrews 1:3, "Who being the brightness of his glory, and the express image of his person, and upholding all things by the word of his power, when he had by himself purged our sins, sat down on the right hand of the majestic on high." So, we can be sure that the glory of Jehovah, which carries and covers the whole earth, dwells in Jesus. The vision of the four beasts of the prophet Daniel confirms this: "I saw in the night visions, and, behold, one like the Son of man [Jesus] came with the clouds of heaven, and came to the Ancient of days, and they brought him near before him, and there was given him dominion, and glory, and a kingdom, that all people, nations, and language, should serve him: his dominion is an everlasting dominion, which shall not pass away, and his kingdom that which shall not be destroyed." And the apostle John, in his Gospel, puts it this way: "And no man hath ascended up to heaven, but he that came down from heaven, even the Son of man which is in heaven" (John 3:13). Jesus is the divine wisdom and quality of holy, holy, holy, who offers holiness to humanity in the shedding of his blood on the cross of Calvary to cleanse the sins of humankind. He extends the kingdom of God from heaven to the earth and within the human body, becoming the promulgator, propitiator, and finisher of holiness.

The reencounter with God is the recovery of holiness by being allotted the benefits we receive in conversion. Holiness is a tool that is included in the package of salvation. It is an instrument of the application of divine properties, through a fact that God makes happen by placing us in Jesus. First Corinthians 1:30 states: "But of him are ye in Christ Jesus, who of God is made unto us wisdom, and righteousness, and sanctification, and redemption." This verse narrates an event that has already happened in the will of God and that no one can alter: we have been placed in Christ Jesus—we are there, we belong to him—and therefore we are creditors of the wisdom, righteousness, sanctification, and redemption of God thanks to Christ Jesus, who brought to us from heaven all the advantages given to assist us on the path of redemption.

In the divine dimension, holiness is an intrinsic property of God. He is holy in existence and transcendence. In the human context, holiness is a characteristic of Jesus (God in the flesh), which we must include in our lives to perfect our nature. It functions as an investor in the balance between the works of the flesh and the fruit of the Spirit. The spiritual balance of the human being in his or her natural state manifests itself with the arm of the works of the flesh dominating our lives. The goal of repentance, forgiveness, justification, adoption, regeneration, and holiness is not to reach a balance between the works of the flesh and the fruit of the Spirit, because the balances are easily broken with the slightest of alterations. The purpose is to reverse the inclination of the arms of the balance totally toward the side of the fruit of the Spirit, so that this new correlation of forces between the carnal personality and the spiritual character cannot be reversed for any reason.

CHAPTER 7

THE CYCLE OF HOLINESS

The cycle of holiness is summarized as follows:

1. God is holy, holy, holy, always has been and always will be, because he is the Source, the example, and the fulfillment of holiness.
2. Adam had holiness by creation, but he lost it.
3. Jesus had holiness by conception, and he never lost it.
4. Humankind acquires holiness by conversion and can keep it or lose it.

Whenever we talk about holiness, we must begin in God, because he is the provider and sustainer of holiness. God is holy, holy, holy, and his holiness remains forever.

God's original and natural creation is holy in substance and in form. The design of the universe was conceived to function in synchronization with God, and this included humanity, which was blessed to be fruitful and multiply on earth and be able to subdue it. Everything God does is holy because it proceeds from his holiness and happens in his eternal time, which is always in the beginning. Nature can be expressed as the function for which and result of which something has been made. God created all that exists to function in harmony with the plan established in his will, following his directives, and seeking the full realization of his purposes within a pure environment of sanctification by both obedience and harmony. But it did not happen like this. Creation went off course because of the disobedience of Adam and Eve. Despite this, God allowed humankind to do everything that he had planned before the beginning. This means that even if Adam had obeyed, the world would have developed as it is today, but without evil, envy, violence, hatred, or wars. Instead, it would be love, peace, and concord reigning among people and nations, and of course we would have avoided many upsets.

We already mentioned at the beginning that Adam enjoyed holiness by creation because he was made of the dust of the earth by the hands of God, who is holy, and had the spirit of life breathed into him by God, who is holy, holy, holy. The destiny of humankind, which is our past, present, and future, could be wonderful, splendid, and comfortable, but because of the loss of holiness and of the relationship with God, we died spiritually and were placed outside his presence. From that fateful moment, it became necessary to recover the holiness to return to original position before him.

God has always been active in his desire to reestablish communication with humankind and has kept that possibility open all the time, offering through many people, at distinct stages of history, the opportunity to recover the holiness by returning to obedience to his commandments. There were many individuals whom God raised up, from Noah to Malachi, but despite their efforts, it was impossible to achieve because of the fallen human condition. All humans failed because of their sinful inheritance, so it was necessary to do something capable of bringing about an internal change that would transform the human spiritual roots to produce fruits of holiness that would be reflected in external conduct. Then, Jesus came.

God made Jesus clean from all sin, without guilt or condemnation. He possessed holiness at conception, or what is the same, was conceived holy. Mary's pregnancy was of divine origin, without any male intervention, to break the condemnation caused by the contamination of human DNA with the transgression of the first created man, Adam. Nowadays, advances in science allow us to take a vegetable seed and inoculate it with substances from external sources to alter its natural genetics, achieving a fruit with distinct characteristics other than those expected. The same thing happened with Adam, the first man on earth: the seed of humankind was contaminated by an external source with disobedience, was inoculated in Adam by the serpent through deception, resulting in the change of human spiritual nature from holy to sinful. The new nature altered by sin has been inherited from generation to generation to the present day because of the contaminated genes, but that did not happen with Jesus, because the genes that he acquired in his miraculous conception in Mary's womb were divine, inoculated by the Holy Spirit and the power of the Highest. In Jesus Christ dwells in all its fullness and splendor the perfect holiness of God. He never lied, hated, offended, or assaulted, and never disobeyed God, but as the Bible says: "And being found in fashion as a man, he humbled himself, and became obedient unto death, even the death of the cross" (Philippians 2:8). Jesus, not for any reason and under no circumstances, lost the holiness that abounded in his life from the miraculous conception. Jesus, having come from holiness, possessed it, showed it, preserved it, and returned it intact and immaculate to where it belongs, the throne of grace, where he is seated at the right hand of the Father in majesty.

Instead of being born like Jesus, human beings must overcome one of the greatest difficulties that can be imagined; we must eliminate the innate sin that inclines us instinctively to deviate from the ways of God. There is nothing we can do to avoid this reality. But it might not have been this way. If Adam and Eve had not sinned, God would have continued to work with us at the same level of communication and direction as he had with them in the garden, and there would have been no need for the incarnation of

Jesus, nor his death on the cross, nor the ministry of the Holy Spirit as we know him today.

One of humankind's similarities to God is related to the Trinity. God is one, composed of three personal characters of the same essence and with the same authority, but with different manifestations and actions: God the Father, Creator and formatore; God the Son, Redeemer and Savior; and God the Spirit, revelator and guider, whereas the human being is a trichotomy (1 Thessalonians 5:23) because he is composed of three levels of consciousness: consciousness of himself (the soul), consciousness of the world (the body), and consciousness of God (the spirit). This similarity makes us subconsciously have the idea that there is something higher. This is the explanation for why, in the oldest civilizations known in all latitudes of the planet, without any biblical knowledge, there is always some kind of rite of worship to a higher being that governs the fate of the world.

Adam's transgression meant renouncing God's spiritual protection and beginning to abide by his own—that is, human—criteria. The instantaneous consequences were spiritual death and the beginning of the fleshly life at our own expense, and the total collapse of humanity. God intervened at that very moment with the first known evangelical sermon, saying: "And I will put enmity between you and the woman, and between your seed and his seed; it will wound you in the head, and you will wound him in the heel" (Genesis 3:15). Until this moment there was friendship between Eve and the serpent, and that relationship led to the consummation of sin, but from there God established enmity between them, to place a protective parameter between humanity and Satan until the seed of the woman (Jesus) arrived, to put the seed of the serpent where it belonged, under her feet.

The first conclusion of knowing everything—"You will be like God, knowing good and evil" (Genesis 3:5)—was the realization that they had made a mistake, and they hid from God. Before obeying the serpent, Adam and Eve knew only good, but after falling into the diabolical trap, they knew the evil, the vicissitudes, and the setbacks of the world and were taken out of the garden. Expulsion is always condemnation, and results in the need to be defended and saved. That salvation can be done only by someone who meets two specific conditions required to save: first, having power to do so, and second, having the will to do so—because someone can have the power to save but not the will to do so, or someone who may want to do it may not have the power to do it. Herein lies the principle of the worship of God, who sent to earth the only person with the power and the will to save us from spiritual death, Jesus of Nazareth, Jesus Christ, the Messiah, the Son of God, the same as God, God himself. Jesus Christ is the only existing method of regaining holiness to reestablish the relationship with God and attain salvation and eternal life.

God's revelation is progressive, not immediate. He first taught faith (Abraham), then showed sin (the law), then called the chosen people to repentance (the prophets) and obedience (holiness), and finally revealed salvation (Jesus Christ). After God's plan of salvation is fulfilled by Jesus on the cross, half-measures regarding holiness and salvation are no longer accepted: either you are holy or you are not holy, or you live in holiness or you do not live in holiness. You cannot be 50 percent holy and the other 50 percent living to please the desires of the flesh and the world. The process to accomplish this is to accept Jesus Christ as your personal Lord and Savior. The holiness that we acquire by obeying the Word of God and following the teachings of Jesus, we must nourish with prayer, fasting, and worship, and take care of it with our testimony of life according to the demands of the gospel. It is not enough to reach Jesus; we must remain subject to his hand until either our departure or his return. The holiness that provides salvation is not a gift, it is a reward for our faithfulness to God, and it gives us back the spiritual characteristic that God requires to reestablish his personal relationship with the human being. This acquired holiness is God's most precious gift because our eternal dwelling place depends on it, and we must make every effort to preserve it.

Holiness not only demands but also bestows. According to the apostle Peter, God provides everything necessary to live in holiness by calling us

1. from darkness to light (1 Peter 2:9);
2. to follow Christ's way of obedience (1 Peter 2:21);
3. to bless instead of curse (1 Peter 3:9); and
4. to gain his eternal glory by way of our obedience (1 Peter 5:10).

But he has also promised us that by living in holiness we will enjoy the following:

1. freedom from the power of sin (Romans 6:14),
2. sufficient grace (2 Corinthians 12:9),
3. the power to persevere (Philippians 4:13), and
4. victory over the enemy (James 4:7).

We may add many more blessings to list.

Holiness is satisfaction for the duty fulfilled, joy for pleasing God, and rejoicing for the unparalleled hope of the spiritual dimension we enjoy in the new life with the inner presence of the Holy Spirit. The inconceivable divine immensity enters the human physical magnitude through holiness. We cannot explain how it happens, but we know it is happening. We do not understand why we feel it, but we are sure we experience it. If we stand firm in Jesus, the unshakable Rock, the cornerstone, we will be safe, but if we falter and fall, we will perish. Let us not hesitate in faith; let us not weaken in prayer; let us not retreat in fasting; and let us continue in perseverance and effort, knowing that God is at the end of the race with the flag at the goal, waiting for us with open arms to give us the reward of eternal life.

04090048-00836281

Printed in the United States
by Baker & Taylor Publisher Services